Monday Morning Motivation

Inspirational Messages That Motivate You to Start Your Week off Right

Tracey,

Be Encouraged!

Be Inspired

Thank you so much for your support"

Monica Marie Jones

Monica Marie J

For more information or to book the author for speaking engagements or book club appearances contact The Literary Loft at: **info@LiteraryLoft.com**.

Author Information:

Monica Marie Jones
http://www.monicamariejones.com
monica@monicamariejones.com

Published By:
The Literary Loft
http://www.literaryloft.com
info@literaryloft.com

Cover Design by Harry Lawson
http://www.enigmagraphics.biz

Edited by Caroline Shiner

ISBN: 978-0-9835509-2-1

Introduction

A New Day

Recently I was talking to a friend and fellow motivator about Monday mornings at his job. He shared that it was the absolute worst time of the week. This was due to the fact that everyone was always upset and depressed because they didn't want to be there. As positive as he is, one can't help but be affected by such negative energy; as it is contagious. Finally, he told me that when my Monday Morning Motivation message pops up in his inbox, it ends up turning his whole day around.

When I decided to do these messages I never could have imagined the impact that they would make. More than one person has shared with me that research shows that suicide occurs more often on Mondays than any other day of the week because of that sense of dread and depression that is often referred to as the "Monday Morning Blues." Each of these readers, who have never met and live in different parts of the world, all said that they feel like these messages are making an impact and a difference when it comes to those statistics. If a little inspiration on Monday morning lifts one heavy spirit or saves one life, then I feel that I have done my job.

I look at Monday in an entirely different way. I truly believe that our health, wealth and how we feel about ourselves depends heavily upon how we perceive things. For example, when I hear the term Monday Morning Blues, I think of how beautiful a blue sky is or that blue is my favorite color as opposed to the negative connotation that the word blue usually holds. Instead of looking at Monday in a dreadful way, I look at it as a new day and an opportunity for a new beginning… as a gift that we are given each week.

I remember when I was a child and I wanted to ask my mother for something, I can't recall what it was, but I prefaced it with, "Mom, when it's 1984 again can I…." She laughed and let me know that years don't come back around like months and days do. We may not be able to get the years back, but there will always be another Monday.

Every day is a new day and an opportunity to start all over again, but I feel that Mondays are the most powerful because they are the beginning.

How often do we think or say that we wish we had the opportunity to do something all over again? Monday gives us that. Today I challenge you to think about ways to make the most of Mondays. I'll start you off with a few, but the rest is up to you…

Re-Commit To a Life-Style Change

Notice that I didn't say diet. Focus on fitness in a way that is manageable and realistic enough for you to maintain for life.

Do Something Differently Than You Did Last Week

Use the weekend as a time to reflect on issues that came up for you throughout the week. Once you've completed that task, use Monday as a day to learn from your mistakes by leaving them behind and moving forward with new goals and action steps.

Begin the Journey of Letting Something Go That Is Not Good For You

Perhaps you want to quit smoking or give up sweets. Monday is a great day to begin and even if you slip up during the week, that's OK because another Monday is on the way for you to give it another try.

Let's make each Monday a new day and if you find yourself getting off track as the week progresses, just remember…another Monday is only seven days away.

How to Use This Book

You are more than welcome to read this book all at once, but for maximum impact it is designed to be read one chapter per week for a year. Read each chapter first thing in the morning every Monday when you wake up, before you do anything else, or as soon as you arrive at the office, before you begin your work for the day.

Apply the topic of the message for each week to your life by focusing on the challenge posed or questions asked at the end of each chapter. Continue to apply and review the concepts, ideas and suggestions that you read in the motivational message for the entire week.

After reading the message, or at the end of the week, reflect on your progress. This can be done alone or with a close friend, family member, co-worker or group. Encourage the person that you share your thoughts with to read the book right along with you. (See the Book Club Guide at the end of the book.)

If you decide to reflect alone, record your thoughts, your answers to the questions, or the action steps that you plan to take to meet the challenges in a journal.

Now sit back, relax and enjoy the read!

Week One

Out With the Old In With the New

No matter when you start reading this book, you are now beginning a brand new year of becoming a brand new you. Think of this as the week before you begin your personal journey of self-care and improvement in every area of your life. This is the last week of your old ways. How will you spend it?

I plan to spend the time cleaning out my space and my life to make room for the new things that I want to receive this year. My issues with clutter usually come to the surface in the way that I manage my clothing and my linens. I buy new things, but I continue to hang on to the old things even if the quality is poor. I keep things that don't fit, things that I never wear or use, and things that I have several duplicate items. I had to ask myself "What is my attachment to these things? Why can't I just let go?"

This practice is similar to how we live our lives. We hold on to people and things that may not necessarily serve a purpose. In essence, they are really just taking up space. It forces me to wonder, what other more useful, valuable and meaningful thing could be in that space that is already taken?

Every household should have staple items. If we narrow it down to just looking at clothing and linens, one major thing comes to mind for me in each category. When the weather gets colder, especially here in Michigan and other places with similar climates, there are a few items that are mandatory. Let's take a literal look at two items: a comforter and a pair of boots. After we look at them literally, then we can liken them to the people and things that we choose to have in our lives.

The primary purpose of a comforter is to keep us warm, but it may also be a security blanket for many. When we personify this, I believe that it is good for us to have one or two people that we can turn to when we feel the need to be comforted. The problem lies in having several people that are comforters in your life. What does this say about you? Are they enabling you? Are you dependent upon them?

Just like with real comforters, one or two good ones will do. Having many more than that means that you probably just use them for show, or they are taking up lots of extra space in your closet. When you have too many people that are comforters, those extra ones are usually 'yes men' or 'yes women'. If someone is always agreeing with you and telling you what you want to hear, how will you ever grow? A true friend or comforter will be caring and kind, but will also always be honest with you and have your best interest in mind.

The purpose of a good pair of boots is to protect your feet by keeping them warm and dry. I have a pair of leather, knee high, kitten heeled boots that I absolutely adore. They are cute, comfortable and they keep my feet warm and dry. The problem is that I wear them so much that I've worn both of the heels off. When I walk on hard surfaces it sounds like I have on tap shoes because where there should be heels on my boots, only exposed metal screws remain.

My mother HATES when I wear shoes that have gotten to that point. She'll say something like, "How can I say this nicely?" Then she will pause for dramatic effect and continue on by saying, "Don't ever wear those boots again." I'm not sure how nice that delivery was, but I can understand where she is coming from.

Since boots cover and protect one of the most important parts of our body, I like to think that they represent integrity. This analogy leads to two important questions…

"What do you stand for?" and "What do you walk in?" Your answer to each of these questions is unique to you, but I'll share my thought process and answers for each.

One of my favorite quotes says, "If you don't stand for something, you'll fall for anything." There are several things that I stand for and tests of my resolve constantly come my way in those areas; therefore, it is important that I stand strong in my beliefs no matter what. My answer to the second question is simple. I walk in faith. If you are walking in anything else, say fear for instance, then perhaps it's time to get a new pair of boots.

This final week of your year of old ways, I challenge you to think about what things and people you need to let go of, and what new things and people you want to attract into your life. Spend this week wisely; it will set the tone for your new year of becoming a new you.

Week Two

Proceed With Confidence

It is our natural human tendency to proceed with caution. This might be necessary when it comes to blatant safety issues such as slippery floors or poorly lit roads, but what is our excuse for proceeding cautiously when it comes to the things that will improve the quality of our lives?

What do you want or need? Is it a new home? A better car? Employment? A mate? Now think about your approach to that thing that you hope for. Are you aggressively and assertively preparing for and or pursuing it, or are you tip toeing around it timidly hoping that it might happen, but secretly sabotaging yourself by not believing that you'll ever truly get it? Or even worse, are you settling for less than what you really want?

Let's combat this by changing our thinking, and our language. Instead of thinking of it as simply a want or a need, think of it as something that you believe that you will receive. Once you are able to wrap your head around that, begin to visualize yourself in that desired situation…

Now that you've got your mind right, it's time to take a look at how you talk. It may simply be a matter of switching out the word "if" for the word "when." Here is an example, "When I get a new car, I'm going to pay for full coverage insurance six months in advance." Isn't that so much more powerful than saying, "If I get a new car, I'm going to try to pay for full coverage insurance, but I might just get no fault insurance at first, because I'm broke." In one simple sentence, you've already defeated yourself before you began.

I don't think we realize just how powerful our words are. What is in our mind comes out of our mouth, and then goes into our ears and right back into our mind. Now if that message is filled with negativity, self-doubt and fear, then look at the sad self-induced cycle that we get caught up in.

Sometimes our hesitation to speak confidently is a result of our worries about how others view us. Don't be driven by what other people might think if your vision doesn't come to pass. It's not about them, but hearing your strong faith may encourage or inspire them. So you very well may be doing them an injustice by not believing in what you want to receive and speaking accordingly.

I've told my mother the things that I'm going to do for her "WHEN I become a millionaire…" so many times that it has changed the way that she thinks and speaks. At her last job she told her co-worker, "I'm only working here until my daughter becomes a millionaire." So as you can see, the boldness and the confidence that are infused in your words and your thoughts are contagious. You are not only setting up your life to receive the things that you believe that you will receive, but you are simultaneously motivating other people to have that same unwavering faith.

This week I encourage you to mentally and verbally claim what is yours. Stop proceeding with caution and begin to proceed with confidence.

Week Three

Trust the Process

I have always tried to control my life. I would subconsciously manipulate situations to work in my favor. I didn't realize that I was doing this until recently. What I found was that while I might have gotten my way for a moment, my master plans often back fired or failed.

For example, when I am facilitating trainings for youth work professionals, I always have one participant that is extremely eager to get to the point of it all right away. What they don't understand is that each workshop agenda has been specifically designed to teach them the new concept or skill in such a way that breaks down and then reveals the pieces in manageable chunks that build upon one another. It's a process often referred to as scaffolding. This method of teaching and learning makes a far more powerful impact than if I had just dumped all of the information on the students at once.

Initially they don't understand why I do things the way that I do, but in the end, a light bulb goes off and it all makes sense to them. When I come across a student like this, I have to remind them to trust the process. My mother always said, "Everything happens for a reason" and I've found that this has always rung true.

Things happen along our journey that are meant to teach us, prepare us, strengthen us and humble us. Let's take relationships for instance. When we meet someone that we are interested in, we try to pour it on thick right up front. We try to make them notice us, like us, or even love us. If they don't, we'll take another approach like trying to play the best friend role in hopes that they will then see how awesome we are and automatically fall in love with us. (I am speaking straight from experience of things that I know I have been guilty of.) Situations like this don't always end in disaster, but here we are again trying to manipulate a situation instead of just relaxing, having faith and trusting that things will happen the way that they are meant to. Perhaps that person was only placed in our lives for a specific reason. That reason may not have been a relationship at all.

The same is the case with our careers, our circumstances…or even when bad things happen. We have to trust the process as opposed to trying to control the situation and manipulate it so that we get our desired result. In doing this we often miss a very valuable lesson or even a blessing that was supposed to come out of what we have gone through. Think about how much more fulfilling an experience would be if we allowed it to run its natural course. We could truly sit back and savor the benefits, knowing that they are ours authentically, not because we manufactured or manipulated the outcome.

This week I challenge you to take a deep restorative breath, sit back, relax, let go and enjoy the ride. Take things one day, one hour, or even one moment at a time. Savor the journey. Allow your life to lead you for a change. Surrender to faith and trust the process.

Week Four

There is Success in Sitting Down

We are always on the go. Multi-tasking has gone from a useful skill to use every now and then, to becoming a way of life. Before we are done with one thing, we are already on to another. Well, I'm sure that we've all encountered a situation that has proven to us that sometimes life has a way of sitting us right on down.

After graduate school I struggled to find full time employment despite my experience and qualifications. Against my will, it was the first time that I had literally and figuratively been forced to sit down in years. It was at that time that I wrote my first book.

You may have lost something dear to you such as a job, your health, an opportunity, or even a loved one. It knocked you right off of your feet and left you asking, "Why me?" Instead of focusing on what went wrong, clear your head and allow for the space and room in your mind and heart that is necessary to receive the gift that is to come out of the sit down situation.

One year at the Essence of Motown Literary Jam and Conference, hosted by the Motown Writers Network, I had the pleasure of hearing bestselling author, Relentless Aaron, give the key note address. He shared how he had been sent to prison for seven years. Most people would have looked at that as the end, but he treated it as a new beginning. During his time of 'sitting down', he wrote thirty books. When he was released, he was offered his first of many opportunities…a fourteen book deal for a quarter of a million dollars.

It's all about how we look at things. Let me use an activity that we do in one of the trainings that I facilitate to drive my point home. I'm going to list a phrase below and I want you to say the first thing that comes to mind based on what you see…

OPPORTUNITYISNOWHERE

What did you see, honestly? The first thing that many people tend to blurt out is "Opportunity is nowhere." But if we simply change our perspective ever so slightly we will see, "Opportunity is NOW HERE."

In essence, it's important that we don't look at setbacks that sit us down as the end. These situations may very well have happened for the specific reason of catapulting us farther than we have ever been before. The next time life sits you down, embrace it and explore the possibilities that you might not otherwise have considered if you were still on the go. There is success in sitting down.

Week Five

An Attitude of Expectation

What do you want? What do you need? Now that you've answered those questions, answer this one…Do you believe that you will get those things?

I'll never forget the day that I auditioned to be a backup dancer for Gospel Recording artist, Kierra 'Ki Ki' Sheard. We'd just found out from our choreographer that Kierra was going to do a ten day, three city tour in Japan and she was looking for one more dancer. As soon as the words came out of our choreographer's mouth, I was already visualizing myself dancing on a stage in Japan. When the day of the audition came, just before we began, I walked over to our choreographer and firmly and confidently said. "I want to go to Japan."

We performed a series of dances for Kierra and I danced, not as if I was auditioning, but as if I was already her dancer on that stage in Japan. Several factors could have made my belief in myself and my ability waver. I wasn't the size that most dancers are. I was nine years older than her and ten years older than the other backup dancer, and I had absolutely no idea where in the world my passport was. I could have defeated myself before I even began.

Kierra watched us intently with a poker face and whispered back and forth with her existing dancer. When we were done she whispered back and forth with our choreographer. The suspense was intense! When she left, he pulled me to the side and whispered, "I hope that you have your passport, because you're going to Japan!" Needless to say, the next day I re-applied for my passport and then a few months later I went on that tour which ended up being an awesome and life changing experience.

This may sound cocky, but I believe that I deserve great things. Each morning I walk to my mail box and my post office box thanking God for the good news that's going to be inside before I even open it. This is actually an accomplishment for me because there was a time where I operated in fear and self-doubt, only focusing on the punishments and karma that I thought would come my way for doing things wrong. I'm sure I wasn't alone and I'm also sure that many of you still think and feel this way.

We don't get what we want because we don't believe that we deserve it.

I've come to the conclusion that the only person that can sabotage or foil any of the plans that I have for what I want to achieve is me. The quickest way for me to do that is by not believing in myself. I constantly visualize everything that I want as already being mine. And slowly but surely, and sometimes quickly, those things begin to manifest in my life.

Let's not confuse expectation with entitlement. I am grateful for and take great care to maintain and sustain the things that I am blessed with by putting in the necessary work to support my faith. It is also important to be aware that when you ask for something, you put it in writing, or you speak it verbally, you just might get it, so be prepared. We often get what we ask for then don't know what to do with it because we aren't ready for it.

As you work to improve your attitude of expectation make sure that you are simultaneously in a state of preparation. If you want a good mate, work to make yourself great. If you want more money, work to strengthen your financial literacy, reduce or eliminate your debt and be a good steward over what you do have. If you want a new job, start investing in new professional attire now. It's all about your attitude. We attract what we give off. It's the same on the flipside; if you are negative or fearful, prepare to receive just that.

This week I challenge you to change your thoughts, actions and attitudes in such a way that you expect amazing opportunities, relationships, experiences and gifts. Believe that great things are yours to be taken... they are just waiting for you to realize it.

Week Six

Let It Marinate

Life is like a piece of meat. To get the most out of this life that we are given, there are certain things that need to be done in order to ensure the best possible flavor, texture and satisfaction. Flavor is all about taste. When you taste something, you experience it, and life is all about experiences. The challenge is making these experiences high quality and meaningful. Texture is all about the feel of something.

In order to live a fulfilled life, we must tend to our feelings in a healthy way as opposed to ignoring them, disregarding them or acting on them before we truly understand them. Satisfaction is the culmination of all of these things because at the end of the day, you want to get the most out of every experience, which will lead to you feeling great about yourself and your life. So the question is: how do we make these things happen? Let's look at how we prepare a piece of meat.

Step One: Clean the Meat

Cleaning out your mind and your life can be as simple as making the time to take a deep, cleansing and restorative breath more than once a day, or as complex as clearing out things and people that may be harmful.

Step Two: Season the Meat

Spice things up! This directly relates to a question that I like to ask myself and others…

"Are you just living your life, going through the basic every day motions to get by? Or are you experiencing life to the fullest by savoring every moment?"

Add some variety. If your level of living is on mild, kick things up a notch or two to medium or hot! Have you been wearing your hair straight with a part on the side for years? Adding the seasoning is as simple as adding some curls or cutting in some layers. Seasoning is about change. What can you do to mix things up?

Step Three: Let it Marinate

One of my signature statements when I teach, speak or facilitate a workshop is, "Let it marinate". This basically means to take some time to let it sink in so that you can process your thoughts, reactions and ideas about a particular statement or experience.

Too often we go through life without stopping to take the time to reflect on our experiences. Reflection is a powerful tool because it helps us to learn and grow by thinking about what went well and what we would change or do differently next time. It also gives us an opportunity to celebrate our successes.

Step Four: Cook the Meat

Cooking the meat represents the actions that we take once we have cleansed, contemplated change, and reflected upon previous experiences. Your cooking, or actions, must be well-planned and timed. For instance, if we cook meat too long it burns or comes out tough. I liken this to when we spend too much time worrying about things that we cannot change or things that are beyond our control. It is also similar to when we sit on an idea or talent too long that we know that we should have released by now to make the world a better place. If we don't cook meat long enough or at the proper temperature, it may come out raw and ultimately make us sick. This parallels our tendency to make decisions and take actions prematurely. It's all about timing. There must be a balance.

I could go on and take this as far as eating, digestion and beyond, but I'll stop at having you consider what the necessary tools are for you to enjoy the dish that is your life. With meat, you'll need a fork and a sharp knife. What utensils will help you to dig in to your life and cut through the literal and figurative clutter?

This week, my challenge to you is to ask yourself the following questions:

What needs to be cleaned up in my life?
What needs to be changed in my life?
What do I need to spend some time mentally processing?
What is my plan of action?
What tools do I need?

① Now let that marinate!

My household needs to be cleaned
up not a lack of respect (from children)
my thoughts are sometimes negative
The way I think of myself sometimes
(not good enough, not doing enough)

②
I need to change the way I see myself,
I need balance as well,

③ I need to mentally process and see
myself successful and when I say successful
happy with myself, happy with my career,
having a more loving relationship with
my children, sister and a significant other,
but most importantly loving myself.

④ My plan of action is to encourage
myself, having a meeting with my children
and sit down and write my sister a
letter,

⑤ I need more of God in my life.
To live in the harmony of God's word.
    I need to grow spiritually
allow the Holy Spirit to clean
me up (mind, body, spirit)

27

Week Seven

Pyramid of Purpose

I love supporting entrepreneurs, but to be completely honest I've always been slightly irritated with the pyramid scheme business model. To my understanding, the basic premise is that the CEO sits at the top and makes all of his or her money by getting people to sign on under them. Those people make their money by getting even more people to sign up as well. I'm sure that this method works for many, but I've never been impressed.

So you can imagine my surprise when someone said that my business of motivating reminded them of a pyramid scheme business model. They pointed out a specific example of how I motivated one person who then went on to motivate another person. In essence, they believe that I have a group of people that I motivate, who then go on to motivate others, and so on. I'd never looked at it that way, but once I was forced to, it didn't seem quite as bad.

In my early years as an educator and social worker, my goal was to save the world. I quickly realized that this was an unrealistic goal. This realization made me take a step back because I found myself getting far too emotionally attached to and involved in the lives of the children and families that I served. Many nights I'd cry myself to sleep at the mere thought of some of the things that my students had to deal with.

In my mind, saving the world may be unrealistic, but it's not impossible. I had to re-evaluate how I could accomplish this without expending so much emotional energy and ultimately burning myself out. This is what brought me to being an author and a motivator.

When you share your gift with the world, you have no idea how far the reach and how powerful the impact can be. Think of yourself as the CEO at the top of your own pyramid of purpose. Whether your audience is your family, your co-workers, your clients, or the general public, know that you are making an impact that reaches farther than you can see. With this being the case, we must operate with integrity, because when you are a person of influence, negativity spreads even more rapidly.

This week, I challenge you to ask yourself a couple of important questions…

What am I passing down from the peak of my pyramid?

Are people genuinely benefiting from what I am offering, or is it ultimately all about me?

As you answer these questions and begin to pass on positivity, keep in mind that a pyramid is nothing without its base or foundation and that the foundation must be strong in order to get to the top.

Week Eight

B Day

On November 1st, 33 years ago, at Cook County Lying -In Hospital in Chicago, Illinois at 1:44 am, I was born to write these Monday Morning Motivational messages for you.

Birthdays are so much more than just a day to celebrate with gifts and loved ones. Birthdays are our own personal New Year's Day. It's a day to reflect and refresh. A birthday is a time to think about where we've been and where we want to go. Within that context, I've decided to declare that November 1st is my B Day, with the letter B standing for far more than just the word birthday. The B represents the things that I like to focus on for my personal new year and I am sure that you will be able to benefit from focusing on these things too.

"B" stands for...

Balance

Having an even work-life balance is key for mental and physical health. You may have heard of the phrase, "Work hard, play hard." This is one mantra that I make sure to adhere to. Often times we spend far too much energy on one side of the spectrum or the other. As a result, other things in our life begin to fall out of balance, too.

I remember hearing someone speak about how a very prominent Pastor schedules his vacation and locks in the date at the beginning of the year before he schedules speaking engagements, business trips, church events or anything else. This is something that we should all do. Don't make play an afterthought. Play is an equally important part of the human experience. Making time to play will rejuvenate you and give you the motivation that you need to give it your all when you get back down to business.

Boldness

One of my new phrases that I like to say is, "Confidence is the new black." When you wear it, it's a really good look. Confidence is not something that you can literally wear externally. You put it on, on the inside, and it's so powerful that it shines right through you and surrounds you with an amazing aura wherever you go. That state of confidence then translates into the action and attitude of boldness. We need to stop walking around here acting like we don't know that we deserve the best in life. With that being the case, we need to know what it is that we want, then not be afraid to ask for it. We need to open our mouths, speak up, and be more assertive. Everything we've ever wanted is already ours, it just needs to be taken or claimed…but to get it we must be bold.

Boundaries

When we don't set clear boundaries, others will set them for us, and I can guarantee that the boundaries that others set will not be in our best interest. We need to begin to set healthy boundaries when it comes to work, family and friends. If we continue to over extend ourselves we will be of no good to anyone and we will be particularly harmful to ourselves. A few years back I wrote a blog in January called, "Happy NO Year" because the best way to begin to set boundaries is by learning to say "No." Even beyond that, we must realize that when we say "No" we don't have to follow it with an explanation. Simply saying "No" is enough.

This week I challenge you to live a balanced life boldly within healthy boundaries. Happy B Day!

Week Nine

Harvest Time

Many seeds are edible. Therefore they serve a dual purpose. They can be eaten and they can be planted. If we eat them they give us satisfaction for a moment, some nourishment, and a limited supply of energy. If we plant or sow them, they will multiply and reap an abundant harvest.

Now think about the seeds that are in your life. What do you do with them? Are you looking for a quick fix or a long term benefit?

The seeds in our lives are our money, time, talents, and energy. Figuratively eating those seeds translates to things like get rich quick schemes, rapid weight loss, and other means of instant gratification. We don't want to wait. We want it all now. What we fail to realize is that by indulging in the small pleasure now, we are actually taking a huge loss in the long run.

Imagine how much more we could have if we planted those seeds. Imagine how infinite the possibilities would be if we invested our money, time, energy and talents into things that would cause them to grow and flourish as opposed to dead end situations, things and people that reap no harvest.

Here is an example of eating the seed versus planting the seed that I want you to consider. Think about which side of the spectrum you are currently operating in, and then think about where you want to be…

You spent $500 in a weekend on an outfit, some shoes, eating out at restaurants, buying drinks, paying cover charges at bars, and parking fees. You looked good, had a funky good time, ate well, and drank well. The next morning you have a headache, perhaps a temporary one from a hangover, or maybe the start of a lingering one from a consequence that was a result of your actions. The fun is over. *You ate the seed.*

You invested $500 in real estate by placing a bid, or going in with a partner to acquire a low cost property in your city. Once you own the property, you rehabilitate it, and sell it for three times more than what you invested, which is still affordable. Now you have simultaneously improved your community, created an opportunity for a family to be home owners and made a profit that you can now invest into something else. *You planted the seed.*

Eating the seed is easy because we believe that it is safe, secure and it feels good right now. Planting the seed is scary because it feels like a risk. Like faith, once we plant that seed, it becomes something that we cannot see immediately...but just because we can't see it, does that mean that it's not there? Taking the planting route may be difficult at times. Things may occur in the process that knock us down or beat us down to the ground, but remember, it is from the ground where all things grow and there is nowhere to go from there but up.

This week I challenge you to plant a seed that you might have otherwise eaten. If you want the harvest, you must sow the seed.

Week Ten

Wardrobe Malfunction

When I was in college, I was a member of the Phi Sigma Pi Co-ed National Honor Fraternity. Each year we would travel to a different state to attend the annual convention. One particular year my roommates and I were in the hallway of our hotel waiting for everyone to finish getting ready for a social event that we'd planned to attend that evening. To pass the time I decided to break out into an impromptu free style dance routine. I did a little move that we might refer to as dropping it like it's hot which basically entailed dropping down into a deep squat and coming back up rather quickly, then repeating that over and over again.

While I was doing this move I was singing a line from the song, Tootsie Roll. "Dip baby dip! Dip baby dip!" Two dips in, the crotch of my jeans ripped from knee to knee. Yes…you read that correctly, I said knee to knee because it burst wide open at the seam in an arc that spanned from one of my knees to the other. When it ripped, it made a popping sound that was so loud that someone came out of the hotel room and said, "What was that noise?" They had heard the sound inside the room even though the door was closed! Needless to say, from that point on my fraternity brothers (as we called each other regardless of gender) teased me by changing the lyrics of the song to "Rip baby rip! Rip baby rip!"

There are three major wardrobe malfunctions that might occur that can turn a lovely day into a devastating one. In addition to a ripped crotch I'd say that the other two most common ones would be a broken heel or a major stain. In my little overactive imagination our wardrobe, or what we wear, represents our life or our business. We come up against setbacks which can be embarrassing or debilitating as well as a major blow to our confidence.

Our heels represent our platform or what we stand for. In business and in life it is imperative that we know what our foundation is and that we stand firmly and strongly upon it. If it is weak, like the broken heel, we will be thrown off balance. We want be able to walk tall but with one broken heel, that will be hard to do. Depending on when, where and how our heel breaks, we may even get hurt. These three things translate to the fact that we must be consistent (balance), operate with integrity (walking tall), and have an intentional plan for maintaining physical and psychological safety (because we might get hurt).

The rip in the crotch represents being exposed. Unfortunately, when it comes to business and life, the better that we do, the more people try to find things that are wrong with us. Now we can try to tie a coat around our waist, which represents hiding, but that won't change the fact that our crotch is still wide open. For that reason, the approach that I've found to be most effective is transparency.

Instead of trying to hide it, I'm more likely to yell, "Hey ya'll, would you believe I just ripped my crotch!" When I train and teach, I've found that people appreciate and relate to honesty. We are not all perfect and we don't always have all of the answers and that is okay; therefore, I recommend authenticity at all times.

I also believe that if anyone is going to drop a big story on me, it's going to be me. You can't blackmail me if I willingly share the information, and if I'm planning on engaging in something that I'm too ashamed to willingly share…then perhaps, I should consider another route. Even if what you've been through carries a stigma or looked down upon, you never know how you are being a blessing to someone else who needs to know that they are not alone.

Finally, a stain on your clothing represents a mistake. As much as we try to avoid them, we all make them and just like certain substances that we soil our clothing with, they are often hard to simply wash away. In such a case, we must look at it as an opportunity to learn.

For example, if I know that my colleague often animatedly talks with his hands, then I know not drink red wine near him when I have on a white shirt. If we look at that from a real life and business perspective it simply means that we try new things, and if they don't work, we use that knowledge to inform our future choices and decisions. Don't waste a moment wallowing in guilt or shame. Take that mistake and count it as a necessary test or trial that was a mandatory prerequisite to your inevitable success.

This week I challenge you to answer the following questions…

What do I stand for?

How can I effectively deal with being exposed (talked about or criticized)?

How can I turn my mistakes into opportunities for learning?

Wardrobe malfunctions are a part of life. Plan accordingly.

Week Eleven

You've Got Me, Who's Got You?

I'll never forget the scene from one of the old Superman movies where Lois Lane was falling through the sky when Superman swooped down, seemingly from out of nowhere, to save her. What was most memorable about that scene for me was what she said,

"You've got me...Who's got you?"

Basically, she wanted know if he was saving her, then who was saving him? That makes me think about many of us who have a tendency to try to save the world at the expense of ourselves. We do this without any super powers and believe that we can come out unscathed. The truth of the matter is that we may not only be hindering the growth of those that we love, but we may also be harming ourselves in the process.

The same is the case with athletic icons. People idolize Michael Jordan, LeBron James, Kobe Bryant and the like, but those men as individuals would not be able to go up against the opposing team to win the game alone. There is a team of people behind them, whose names we may not even know, that support them on the path to victory.

Are you a self-appointed superman or superwoman, always flying to the rescue of those in need around you? If so, who is looking out for you?

Even the man of steel has a weakness...kryptonite. Kryptonite is the only thing that can weaken and ultimately kill the otherwise invincible man. If this seemingly invulnerable man has something that can take him out, then why do we feel that we are exempt? Your kryptonite may come in the form of physical or mental illness, loss or grief, or unexpected hardships that come your way. Or, quite simply, life and all of the responsibilities that you've taken on will eventually wear you down. Because of this reality it is important that you have someone or something to rescue you too.

So, the question is...Who's got you?

The first step is simple. Let God do His work. You may think that you can save the world, but the first thing that I quickly learned as a social worker is that you can't. Of course, we can make a difference and an impact in many major ways, but we must face and accept the fact that no matter how hard we may try, we cannot save the world. If you truly want God to move in your life and the lives of others...then get out of His way.

The next step is to identify a sturdy support system. This is a network of people that serve as a safety net that can catch you when you fall or a scaffold that can assist you in reaching higher heights. This can vary from an army of one, to a starting lineup of five or an all-star dream team of twelve or more. Find people that add value to your life in that they have strengths in areas where you are weak. These are people that have the strength and wisdom to steer or pull you away from substances and situations that might destroy you.

This week I challenge you to take a step back and observe your behaviors and habits when it comes to trying to be everyone's everything. The next time you are in the midst of saving someone, imagine them turning to you and saying, "You've got me…Who's got you?"

Week Twelve

Beyond the Advance

As soon as trouble comes, we want to be rescued right away. When we are working at something, we want the payment before the work has been completed. Therefore, it is safe to say that most of the time we want all of the rewards, answers and solutions for our problems and our work right up front.

We settle for Mr. or Misses Right Now. We take credit cards and loans with high interest rates. We want to lose ten pounds in ten days. We devour fast food while on the go. What we often fail to think about is what this obsession with expediting our life, experiences and allowances might actually cost us. If you are going through some type of trial right now, you probably want the answer, the victory, or you just plain old want things to get better immediately…but sometimes, waiting until after the storm to see the sunshine and the rainbow makes it worth the wait.

Talented authors and musicians often get hefty monetary advances for book and record deals. This means that they get a lump sum of money up front, which will be made back once their books or records begin to sell. It seems like a sweet deal, and quite often it is, but, if the advance is not made back in sales, then the artist does not receive anything above and beyond it. They do not get the overflow.

An advance may sound like the best thing since sliced bread, but let's look at it from another angle…

When I visited the "And Still We Rise" exhibit at the Charles H. Wright Museum of African American History in Detroit, the charismatic tour guide led us through each area and taught us tons of interesting facts that confirmed for me how much our history informs our present state of being.

In 1862 the current president, Abraham Lincoln, issued an executive order to free slaves. It was called the Emancipation Proclamation. Sadly, many slaves never experienced true freedom because their owners had another plan in mind. Most of the slaves were held because of the debt that they owed to their masters. The owners had the audacity to say that since they provided food, clothing and shelter for the slaves, that they had to work off that debt before they were truly allowed to be free.

Upon hearing this I made an immediate correlation between the happenings around the Emancipation Proclamation then, and the music industry now. Artists are given weighty advances, fancy cars, clothing and jewelry upon signing a record deal. The allure of it all prompts eager singers and rappers to sign thick contracts without reading the fine print. Once the album drops and millions of copies are sold, the rising star is left wondering why they are seeing little to no profit from all of their hard work.

What they fail to realize is that they are in fact paying for all that they were afforded in advance. The company deducts the advances and expenses from the profits made from the units sold.

So very similar to the situation with the slaves, we may think that we have made it big time by getting big things quickly, but what we are really faced with is a big time disappointment as we work to repay a debt that we never asked for in the first place. All of this goes to show that in many instances; up front advances, quick fixes and easy answers come at a much higher cost.

Now that I've got you thinking, I want you to relate this to your life. I want you to think about how when we have a problem, we want the solution right away. We may get that answer or incentive, and it may be good, but what we don't realize is that what we could have gotten on the other end is far more valuable. We don't go through anything in vain. Everything that we experience is for a reason. As soon as things go wrong, we run to God and want him to fix it on the spot. If He does not, we get upset and feel that He does not hear our cries. We don't trust Him, so we look for that quick fix instead.

If we just trust Him and wait to get through something, then we will come out in the end equipped with strength, patience and knowledge in addition to a desired income that will exceed our expectations. Since we've put in the hard work, the sweat and the tears…the payment that we receive, or the solution to our problem is so much more savory. Sometimes we just have to wait patiently to see what is beyond the advance. Why settle for good when you can have great?

If the answer to your problem is not coming as quickly as you would like, it's okay! Know that an even sweeter deal is on the way.

Week Thirteen

Shed the Skin You're In

Every now and then there comes a time where we need to leave old things behind. Comfort makes it so that we don't want to let go, but sometimes letting go is necessary in order for us to grow.

Think about that pair of jeans that you love. It may be too big, it may be too small, it may be worn and tattered...either way it's beyond time to get a new pair. We hold on to it because it's what we know and it fits us, or at least used to fit us just the way we like it. Jeans that are too tight sometimes even stretch with us as we grow because we wear them so much. We think that new jeans just wouldn't be the same. Then one day, you're out in public and the button pops off, or the zipper breaks, or the inseam rips. We wait until some major upheaval occurs before we finally give in and say, it's time for a new pair.

This is much like our lives. Many times we stay in a situation because it's comfortable, it's what we know, and it seems safe...but if we stay in that same place...how will we ever grow? It makes me think about snakes. According to wisegeek.com, "Snakes shed their skin to allow for growth, as well as to remove parasites along with their old skin." Think about that for a moment.

If we are trying to symbolically stay in our old skin, it binds us so that we cannot grow. Our old skin has also accumulated parasites and other harmful things which we need to rid our system of. Those parasites could represent things like bad habits or behaviors that we need to turn away from.

Once a snake goes through the shedding process, its old worn scales are replaced with new healthy skin. This can occur anywhere from every few weeks to once a year. When you think of the skin that you need to shed, it can range from simple to complex. It may mean donating all of the old clothes that you no longer wear and replacing them with new clothes. Or it may mean walking away from a very comfortable yet stagnant or difficult situation.

In order to successfully shed the skin that you're in, it is important to be honest with yourself. We often make excuses and try to convince ourselves that we are just fine where we are, but if we look at the situation truthfully and honestly we will find that we may in fact be hanging on to layers upon layers of old skin. We also tend to wait for something to happen (Like the jeans ripping that I mentioned earlier) to give us that push or that reason. We don't need an excuse to grow. The fact that it's just due time should be reason enough.

Once the old skin has been shed...leave it behind. When snakes leave their skin behind, it is still intact, but you don't see them turning back to try to squeeze into their old set of scales, do you? They move on and continue going through life with the new healthy skin.

When was the last time you shed the skin you were in? This week, I encourage you to take a good hard look at yourself and determine if there are some layers that need to be shed.

Week Fourteen

Take Your Medicine

A while back I made a spur of the moment decision to attend a literary conference in Kansas City, Missouri. I immediately paid for the conference and my hotel room in advance to make sure that I didn't change my mind. After researching the price of flights I'd decided that I'd rent a car and drive the thirteen plus hours all on my own. On the day of the trip, I realized that based on how busy my week leading up to the trip was and how demanding my week after the trip would be, that I'd gotten myself into a pretty ambitious undertaking.

I must admit that as the trip neared, worry and anxiety began to set in as I faced the reality of finances, time and the fact that I was tired and trying to beat a cold. As much as I am a cheerleader for faith, I began to waver and I wasn't quite sure how I would pull this trip off, if I could make it happen at all. However, I prayed. In response I simply heard, "Trust Me."

A concerned friend began to go back and forth with me about how it wasn't safe for me to drive that long distance alone. So after arguing that I was a trooper because I had driven that distance and longer on my own several times, I decided to at least check to see if there were any good deals on last minute flights. As I looked over all of the outrageous prices, it occurred to me to check on the status of my frequent flyer miles to see if I was eligible for a reward flight.

A reward flight to Kansas City would cost me 25,000 frequent flyer miles. I had 25,009. On the day that I was schedule to hit the road, I was able to book a FREE, non-stop, round trip flight that was only two hours in duration as opposed to the thirteen plus hours that I would have had to drive one way. It was clear to me that this leap of faith was one that I was meant to take.

This particular conference was filled with some of my favorite authors. These were famous authors that I'd grown up reading, authors that have made the New York Times and Essence Bestsellers lists on multiple occasions. I whisked in and greeted them all personally as if they had been family that I hadn't seen in a while, and they embraced me equally so. Well into the long Saturday full of workshops, panels and intense conversations, I realized that I was so engaged, that not a single worry had crossed my mind.

I was so into what I was doing that the things that usually occupy my thoughts such as finances, relationships, responsibilities, and concern for family had not even attempted to enter my mind. It was at that very moment that I came to understand a simple truth that can help and heal us all of the toxic feelings of worry, fear and anxiety.

Being immersed in what you love makes you forget about the things that aren't right in your life. It erases your worries and allows you, if only for a moment...to be free. It's like the serum to personal freedom. It is a feeling like no other...one that we should be intentional about making happen in our lives on a regular basis.

The remedy is simple...

Identify It

Identify the thing or things that you truly love and are passionate about.

Create It

Create regular experiences or opportunities for yourself where you are immersed in that thing that you love.

Capture It

Savor the experience while you are in it, and capture it so that you can revisit it if you need to. This can be done through taking notes, journaling, taking pictures or reflecting on the experience afterward.

This week I challenge you to set aside some time to immerse yourself in that hobby, that project or that class. Take that trip. Spend time with that person. Whatever it is for you, make it happen, if only for a moment, and watch how you will be almost instantly alleviated of the day to day woes that often plague your heart and your mind.

Worry, fear and anxiety are the illness. The antidote is immersing yourself in what you love. Get healthy. Get happy. Get whole.

Week Fifteen

You Are the Boss of You

We have a tendency to torture ourselves. We overbook ourselves. We take on more than we can handle. We help other people more than we help ourselves. Do any of these behaviors sound familiar?

What I have eventually come to realize is that in the past I made my life a lot harder than it had to be. Sometimes we take our lives and ourselves way too seriously. As an entrepreneur, I am my own boss...but as people, we are all the bosses of our own lives. Therefore, we have the power to make our lives work for us.

How can you adjust your daily routine to reduce unnecessary stress? Here are a couple of simple suggestions...

Pay Yourself First

When I say this, I don't just mean money. Time and energy are just as valuable as money. Do something for yourself first, before you begin to think about what needs to be done for the children, what needs to be done around the house, or what you need to do for work. Each day, I exercise first, which sets a nice tone for the rest of my day and helps me to have more energy, less stress, and peace of mind in knowing that I took care of myself first.

Taking care of yourself first doesn't have to take hours. It may just be that you spend the first five minutes of your day in prayer, enjoying your favorite breakfast, or reading a chapter of a juicy novel. When we neglect ourselves and put all of our energy into others, resentment begins to creep in and take over our joy. When you put yourself first you will feel much better about the things that you do for everyone else.

Make Time for Fun

Some people play too much, but most people don't play enough. Play is an integral part of the human experience. So make some time for fun, or those things that you've always wanted to do. Reintroduce spontaneity into your life.

Go to a carnival, arcade or movie with your mate. Read a book for enjoyment instead of business or school. Make a spur of the moment decision, throw caution to the wind and just do it!

This week I challenge you to come up with a simple and manageable plan to make your life work for you. You are the boss of you, so take charge and adjust accordingly.

Week Sixteen

Experience Life

I think while I sleep. My mind continues to work long after I am deep within slumber's grasp. This is why I sleep with two journals and my laptop in the bed next to me and a pen on the night stand. This quote woke me up out of my sleep on Sunday morning...

"Live to experience, not to avoid...but do so in such a way that the mirror is your friend and not your foe."

We spend a lot of time in life suspended in a state of avoidance. We live to avoid what is often inevitable instead of savoring moments, engaging in experiences, appreciating the arts, enjoying relationships and celebrating life.

In trying to avoid things, most of which are beyond our control, we expend the majority of our energy, which is a precious resource that is only borrowed and at some point must be given back.

We don't let people get close to us; especially the ones that we might really care about or potentially fall in love with, to avoid being hurt.

We don't take on or tackle the careers or the professional goals that we have in order to avoid failure.

We don't ask for what or who we want to avoid being rejected.

Essentially we torture ourselves by constantly operating in avoidance mode as opposed to being present and in the moment...instead of fully experiencing life right now. When I say experience life, I don't mean going straight buck wild. We have to be able to live with our choices and decisions. A guest pastor that spoke at church said, "We go to bed with one of two things, results or regrets." Which one sounds like the better bed mate?

In experiencing life we have to be able to look ourselves in the mirror, hence the second part of the quote above.

This past weekend I made the conscious decision (and a pact with a friend) to begin to experience life to the fullest. There is so much out there to love, but we often don't even realize it because of our tendency to focus on the negative. The very thing that we are trying so hard to avoid may be the very thing that is the key to our breakthrough. It all comes down to trusting the process. We get so wrapped up in the outcomes that we miss the best parts of life...the process...the experience.

This week I challenge you to let go of your need to control everything in order to avoid what you don't want to happen. I challenge you to focus on the experience of life.

Week Seventeen

Please Pass the Activator

Ok, let's be honest…out of everyone that is reading this, who had or knows someone who had a Jheri Curl? For my younger subscribers who were born after the eighties, this might be a foreign term to you. If so, simply do a Google search of the phrase "Michael Jackson with Jheri curl" and you should find a plethora of pictures and definitions. According to Wikipedia, "The Jheri curl is a hairstyle that was common and popular in the African American community. Invented by and named for Jheri Redding, the Jheri curl gave the wearer a glossy, loosely curled look."

Now don't get it twisted. That glossy shine by no means came easy. The harsh mixture of chemicals that were needed to make this look possible often left the user's hair in an extremely brittle and dry state. In order to bring those juicy curls to life, Michael Jackson and all of those that followed suit with the popular hairstyle from the 1980's had to add a product called activator.

Now think about that major dream, vision or goal that you have for your life. Can you picture it? Some of you may be living it right now, but for many of you, it is only a dream, vision or goal in your mind or on paper that has no life. So what's the difference? What is missing? What do those that are living in their dreams have that the rest of you do not? The secret ingredients are faith and belief. Until you add those things to your dreams…they are dead. You need faith and belief to bring your goals to life. Faith and belief are the activators that add the juice to your vision, thus making it a reality.

These two ingredients create an activator that gives your dreams that shine. Your goals no longer lie dormant, dull and lifeless.

If you don't have the activator, you may as well not speak about it.

If you don't have the activator, you may as well not write about it.

If you don't have the activator, you may as well not waste time daydreaming about it or visualizing it.

Sometimes we are not even aware that our style is dry and crunchy.

We say things like, "I really want to go to back to school BUT…"

"I really want this job BUT…"

You might as well finish those sentences with, "…BUT….I don't believe." Or "BUT…I don't have faith."

We defeat ourselves with our little faith and lack of belief before we even begin. If you find yourself speaking in such a way, it's time to get some activator!

When a loved one or a friend is in a drought, don't have them walking around looking like that! You would not let someone that you truly cared about walk around in public with their hair all over their head looking all crazy. So don't allow your people to kill their dreams by not believing that they will come to pass. Give them a little squirt of your activator. Share how it has brought the shine back into your life. Share your faith and belief-based activator until they are able to stock up on their own supply.

Not too long ago I heard a quote that really resonated with me. It said, "When your focus is clear, what you want will show up in your life, but only to the extent that your focus is clear." Let me amend that twice over for the purposes of this message.

"When your faith is strong, what you want will show up in your life, but only to the extent that your faith is strong."

"When you believe, what you want will show up in your life, but only to the extent that you believe."

1 Part Faith + 1 Part Belief = Activator

(The activation of your vision, your goals and your dreams)

Don't just get a few squirts or one bottle of activator…invest in an unlimited lifetime supply.

Week Eighteen

A Ph.D. in Me

I have two degrees, two certifications and years of practice in my fields of study...but there has been no better teacher, lesson or education than life. I went straight from Kindergarten through graduate school without any breaks, other than summer vacations during grade school and then one summer semester off after my first year of college. After having been engaged in formal education for so many years, I thought that life without school might feel foreign. I was wrong. I have probably learned more in the eight years that I have been out of school than I did during the eighteen years that I was in school.

Over those long school years I learned a whole lot about many different things, much of which I have forgotten. It wasn't until I had completed graduate school and stepped out into the real world that I came to realize that I didn't know a whole lot about me.

Higher education establishments put together degree programs that have specific classes that you must take in order to graduate in your selected major or area of study. There are certain courses that must be taken before you are allowed to take others, these are called prerequisites. There are also classes that you must take that have nothing to do with your major so that you are well rounded. These are called basic studies. The classes that you take that dig deep into your area of study through practice or a more specific focus are called practicums, labs, and methods courses. If you want to take a course on your own without actually attending a class with your peers, it's called an independent study.

School was great, and it was an experience that I wouldn't trade, but I believe that we can have an equally awesome experience by putting together our own personalized degree program. A program that I like to think of as a Ph.D. in ME.

Ph.D., which stands for Doctor of Philosophy, and is also referred to as a Doctorate Degree, is the highest degree that one can earn.

Think about it. You can set up your own personal degree program based on your interests, passion and purpose. The world is your University. Your recommended or required readings and assignments might include books, travel, movies, relationships, conferences, seminars and networking events that you select based on the things that you enjoy, as well as your plans and your goals.

Now let's take the format that Colleges and Universities have created and break down a few of these key concepts so that you can begin to create a program that helps you get to know yourself and improves the quality of your life.

Pre-Requisites and Basic Studies

These represent those things in your life that you may need to put in place before you are able to comfortably and successfully move to the next level. For example, as I continue to build and grow my business, I have found it necessary to get my personal finances in order first. There are certain basic things in your life that must be done before you move on to higher level things or they will keep holding you back or getting in the way. In many cases, these things teach you or prepare you so that you are equipped to move forward and upward. What do you need to do in order to lay the foundation for your future?

Practicums and Labs

These are symbolic of the actual hands-on experiences where you get out and try things. This may be diving into writing and publishing your own book, or trying your hand at a new talent or skill such as singing or painting. I've found that sometimes the best way to learn is to just get out there and give it a try. We can only learn so much from reading books and listening to lectures. The most powerful type of learning comes when the student is fully engaged in the experience.

My literary mentor, Sylvia Hubbard often says, "Just go in there and try to break it." in reference to learning the latest technology. When my brother was younger, he used to take things apart to find out how they worked. Sometimes breaking things and making mistakes is the best way to learn. What are some of the areas of your life where you need more hands-on experience?

Independent Study

I often meet many new people and speak to and teach large crowds. I've come to learn that as much as I am surrounded by people, I need to spend as much, if not more, time alone. Time alone not only gives me the balance that I need, but it's also a time to rest, reflect, recharge and do research. While a huge part of your personal degree program comes from the relationships that you build with others...the relationship that you build with yourself is just as important. How much intentional "Me" time do you set aside?

Assignments

Give yourself homework. This includes listing and setting goals for books that you want to read, people that you want to meet, events that you want to attend, places that you want to travel to, fears that you want to overcome and new things that you want to learn or try. These assignments can come in the form of long term and short term goals, or daily tasks that you check off on your to-do list. What does your self-made syllabus or custom made curriculum consist of?

Professors

Everyone should have at least one mentor. I would even go as far as to recommend that you have a mentor in every area of your life. For example, a spiritual mentor, a professional mentor, and a health and fitness mentor. The choice is yours, but you should always have someone that you can look to, no matter their age, to help guide you to where you want to be. Unlike college professors, these mentors aren't just there to lecture to you. They should model the skills and behaviors that you aspire to, provide opportunities for you, and answer your questions. Who are your mentors?

CLEARLY I could go on and on with the metaphors...but I'll stop here to give you a chance to let it all marinate in your mind. This week, or month, or season, or year I challenge you to create your own program where you first learn about YOU; and then become the best YOU that you can be. Join me as I obtain my Ph.D. in ME!

Week Nineteen

What is Your Escape Plan?

When I go out to do observations and quality assessments for youth programs, one of the first things that we look for is their emergency procedures, which should be posted in plain view. Emergency procedures let people know which way to go and what to do in order to stay safe in the midst of chaos.

We've become so desensitized that we fail to realize that we are in the midst of a state of emergency. When we look at the messages in the media and popular culture, the literacy rate, the economy, mental illness and all of the things that are going on around us, it's a wonder that we haven't all given up.

Since we are in such a state, we need a plan of escape in order to keep our sanity. Here are some procedures that I suggest you practice in order to keep you grounded, balanced and essentially safe...

Self-Care

I've begun to spoil myself because with all of the work and travel that I do, I need to re-build, re-energize and replenish regularly. I get professional massages, pedicures, hairstyling, eye brow arching and personal fitness training on a regular basis. During times when I am trying to cut back or save money, I do all of these things myself.

This is a huge change because a few years ago I hardly ever treated myself to any of these things that I now consider necessities. I consider them as such because in order to continue to give my gift to the world in the way that God wants me to, I need to make sure that my cup is not only full, but overflowing. What do you, or can you, do to increase your focus on self-care?

A Financial Plan

I've come to realize that poverty is a mindset...one to which I have been trapped in for many years and still struggle to be released from the grips of. If we are not focused on financial literacy, we tend to spend more than we save, give more than we have, and live well beyond our means, often struggling from pay check to pay check. Now is the time to begin to think about how you might get your finances in order in such a way that you are prepared for the emergencies that can and do emerge every day. Even if it is as simple as an old school piggy bank, put aside a little money every day and invest in something that will yield a return. In what ways can you strengthen your financial practices?

A Confidante

Quite simply, you need someone that you can talk to or confide in. You need someone that you can talk to who you can trust and that is an active listener. When I say active listening I mean not just hearing what you are saying, but truly listening, remembering, empathizing, knowing when to be silent and knowing when to practice self-control. We don't always want someone to offer the solutions, the lectures, or the shoulda's, ought to's, and need to's....we simply need someone who will just listen without judgment, yet be honest and hold us accountable for the goals and plans that we share with them. Who is your confidante? If you don't have one, identify one...if no one meets the requirements...God is always on deck.

A Place of Peace

In an actual emergency, this would be a fallout shelter or some other place that would keep you safe in the midst of a natural disaster or act of terror. The things that we deal with in our everyday lives are just as real and we often need to take cover to reflect and regroup.

It's also important to keep in mind that your environment has a huge impact on your state of mind. I've noticed that my physical environment often reflects my mindset. When I am at peace, my space is clean, organized and creatively decorated. When I'm out of sorts, my place looks like it has been hit by a tornado. If you don't have access to a little cabin or some other serene get away, then your home or at least one space in your home should be your place of peace.

Designate a spot, or if you have a loft like me where everything is in one big space, design it in a way that brings you the serenity that you need. I like to use aroma therapy candles and fragrant incense to set a serene mood. As much as possible, keep your space clean and clutter free. I personally discourage unannounced or uninvited guests because I know that's what I need for my own sanity. Pick your space, design it to your liking and set your standards and boundaries. Everyone should have their very own place of peace to retreat to in tumultuous times.

This week I encourage you to write, or mentally devise, the first draft of your emergency procedures or escape plan.

What are your top three self-care practices?

What is your financial plan?

Who is your confidante?

Where is your place of peace?

Write them, type them, put them on a poster board....do whatever works best for you and post them in plain view.

There is no need for a drill like those we used to do in school to practice what we might do in the event of an emergency because the time is now. Devise your escape plan and your emergency procedures and practice them regularly.

Week Twenty

What Were You Born to Do?

One Sunday when I was in church a couple gave a powerful testimony that moved me to tears. The wife had been stricken with a severe heart condition that rewound her life and abilities back to infancy. She couldn't walk, talk, or do any of the basic things for herself that we often take for granted. Her husband did everything in his power to take care of her. During that time she asked him, "Does it bother you to have to take care of me so much?" He answered, "No, this is what I was born to do."

In life we often settle for less than we are capable of and less than we deserve. When it comes to what we are capable of, we find comfort in what we are good at instead of pushing further and finding out what we are great at. It may be a skill or talent, but then it may be something as simple as caring for a loved one; as was the case with the story above. So I ask you, "What were you born to do?" You may not know now and you may not find out until later in life, like the husband did with his wife's illness; but in the meantime, are you pushing past the good, exploring what you are great at and operating in that with excellence?

Now, let's take a look at what you deserve. We are so quick to play the role that looks like this: "If anyone must suffer, if anyone must come last, if anyone must go without....then let it be me." A dear friend of mine used to go through life saying and living under that belief only to come to the realization that it was false humility. According to Wikipedia, 'false humility' is the act of "...deprecating one's own sanctity, gifts, talents, and accomplishments for the sake of receiving praise or adulation from others."

Don't you know that you deserve the best? No matter where you've been, no matter what you've been through, no matter what you've done, at the end of the day you deserve that mate that loves you unconditionally. You deserve that job, career, salary, or grant that you've always wanted. You deserve to be in the best of health mentally and physically. Know your worth! Just as you were born for a specific purpose, someone else was born for a specific purpose for you.

So when it comes to relationships, don't just settle for who loves you, no matter how they treat you...someone was born just to be the love of your life that you deserve, if you wait patiently and faithfully. When it comes to your health, and you think there is no way out, know that there was a doctor that was born just to save your life, or a friend that was born just to pray and encourage you, keeping your spirits high until you heal. Your children may have been born to slow you down, give you someone to love and cherish, and then ultimately someone to take care of you when you can no longer care for yourself.

When people call on me for a word of encouragement, or thank me for a message that I wrote that spoke to their situation, I feel like I'm just doing my job, because I know…this is what I was born to do.

Whatever life has thrown your way or taken away, know that there is a specific purpose for which you were born and on the flip side there is someone, or more than one person that was born to help you or see you through.

What were you born to do?

Who was born for you?

Week Twenty One

Life is Like a Football Game

I had a personal wakeup call this weekend when a friend unknowingly brought one of my behavior patterns to my attention. I came to realize that I have a tendency to brush certain things off, saying or acting like I don't care or like things don't affect me in situations where they should or do. This got me to thinking, is this a defense mechanism that I subconsciously use to avoid being hurt or disappointed?

It made me think of football. In the little that I understand of the game, I know that you either play offense or defense. The defense defends the ball and the offense goes after the ball. According to Wikipedia, "The objective of the game is to score points by advancing the ball into the opposing team's end zone." I relate this to life.

Another word for offense is attack. Do you find yourself taking life head on, attacking challenges and obstacles or goals and dreams? Or, do you play it safe by going through life trying to defend your mind, your heart and your ego by manipulating situations so that there is little to no risk...so that you can't get hurt...so that you cannot fail. We often spend most of our time defending ourselves from other people. We don't want them to talk about us. We don't want them to disappoint us.

We place so much on and in people. But do you know that people talking about you has prepared you for your impending greatness? Do you think that the numbers of naysayers will decrease as your success, prosperity, and popularity increases? In all actuality, it is just the opposite. A person talking about you is all a part of your preparation because when you get better, it only gets worse.

People begin to look and dig for something to talk about and if they can't find it, they will create it. So if you weren't or aren't used to it, you might not be able to handle it. If you hadn't experienced it, it might take you out. It might make you want to quit. It might make you want to hide. If you had not been through something, you might not be able to handle all that is coming along with your victory. Your trials have strengthened you and humbled you in preparation for the greatness that is before you.

People will leave you. People will betray you. People will disappoint you. Don't be discouraged! You've experienced what you've been through to prepare you for what God wants you to do. Because now you KNOW that you can make it...because you HAVE made it. And you know that people are just that...people...not perfect...not God. So why even play yourself by expecting so very much of them. Most are hurting...and they need you. They need you to operate in your God given gift to help heal them.

Now let me reverse up off of that tangent I just went on to drive my point home. What are you spending your valuable time doing? What side of the ball are you on? Are you playing defense, to avoid pain, hurt, disappointment, failure and a host of other things that are all a part of life, and perhaps very important pieces of your preparation for greatness? OR are you playing offense by attacking every obstacle that comes your way, whether good or bad, all making you stronger, right and ready for the tasks that lay before you?

Life is like a game of football. What position do you play?

Week Twenty Two

Every Wall has a Window or a Door

Every summer I take a vacation to visit my older brother at his beautiful historic home in Springfield, Massachusetts. One year I noticed that there was a door in the room where I slept each night that I hadn't used and I wasn't sure where it led to so I asked him about it. He explained to me that it led out to the family room before saying, "Every wall in this house has a window or a door." As simple as that sounds, I found it to be quite fascinating. It made me think about how it could be a perfect analogy for how we view our lives.

In life, we come up against many obstacles, barriers, or walls. These walls might be things like financial hardship, relationship related heartache, neglect, abuse, health issues or loss of prized possessions or loved ones. More often than not, even though they are walls that we cannot literally touch or see, we tend to look at them as very real set-backs or dead ends. Since we cannot see these obstacles with our eyes, why not throw in a bit of blind faith and believe that each wall that we come up against has a window or a door.

Now that I look back and mentally picture the design of my brother's house, every wall really did have a window or a door. All of the windows were portals to the outside world, as was the front door and back door, but the remaining doors led to other rooms or closets.

With some obstacles, the way out is clear, as is the case with windows and front, back or side doors. Those obstacles that we face that feel too hard to get through may have been one of those doors that lead to another room or a closet. When you come to a barrier that has a door that leads to another room, this is representative of a barrier that has been put in your life to lead you in another direction, or show you another way.

When you are at a wall and the door leads to a closet, perhaps this represents that there are some things that need to be stored or tucked away. Hence, some barriers in your life are meant to teach you valuable lessons that you are to store in your mental arsenal to use at another time or to help others get through what they are going through.

This week I challenge you to look at the obstacles in your life differently. The next time you come to what seems to be an impenetrable wall in your life, know that there is a window or a door and take some time to think about what type of door it may be. If there seems to be no way out, there will always be another way or a lesson to be learned.

Week Twenty Three

Get Out of Your Own Way

Take a moment to envision where you want to be in life. Where do you want to live? What do you want to look like? How do you want to feel emotionally? What kind of car do you want to drive? How much money do you want to make? What do you want the state of your business to be? What do you want for your family?

Now, think about the thing or things that are holding you back from where we want to be. If we are completely honest with ourselves we will admit that our largest obstacle is often the person that we look at in the mirror every day.

There are several ways that we get in our own way. The most obvious way is our lack of belief in our own abilities which allows fear, doubt, negative self-talk and procrastination to dictate our futures. If we do that, we know it…but I want to call out some of the other hidden and sometimes subconscious things that we do to sabotage ourselves.

Burning the Candle at Both Ends and in the Middle

When you have a vision or a goal that you've set for yourself, it's a natural tendency for those that are driven to want to grind and give it all we've got. The problem is that sometimes we go so far that we not only give it all we've got but we give it what we don't have as well.

I remember the first and only time that I ever ran out of gas in my car. I was ripping and running all day, and I actually had the money. I was just so busy pushing my agenda to the limit that I never set aside the few moments that it would take to refuel. So as a result, there I was, in the middle of the freeway, at midnight, out of gas. At this point, not only was I held back, I was brought to a screeching halt. I went from doing too much to not being able to do anything at all.

There are two things to keep in mind if this sounds like you. First of all, you won't be good to anyone or anything if you are burnt out mentally, physically and emotionally. That purpose or calling that has been placed on your life will be placed on hold and you will be placed on a stretcher or a hospital bed. And finally….challenge God and allow him the opportunity to show you all that He can do for you. Trust that He's right there next to you on the battle field of life. Faith takes work, but even God rested.

Talking About What You Can't Do and Doing What You Don't Want to Do

I saw author, ReShonda Tate Billingsley speak one day and one of the many things that she said that stood out to me was, "Every minute spent talking about what you can't do is a minute that could be spent doing it." This rings so true! We spend SO much time talking about what we can't do and why we can't do it. Those minutes, hours, days and weeks could be spent taking action on the plan that is burning inside of us.

On the same note, we often spend just as much time doing things that we know we don't want to do. Perhaps it's that job that you hate and you know that deep down in your heart, if you step out on faith and leave it, God will have something even greater waiting for you. Maybe it's all of those things that you do to help others reach their goals and realize their dreams…which is great…but what about you?

Start thinking of your moments as money in a bank account that will disappear if you don't spend it or invest it. Think of every hour as one million dollars. You get the same amount each day, Twenty-four million dollars, and how you use it is up to you. Will you use it wisely? Will you waste it? Or will you go too hard with it and fall into burning that candle at both ends and in the middle?

There are several other factors that contribute to you getting in your own way...getting in the way of that future that you want. These factors include the company that you keep, your willingness to give, how you manage what you are given and so on. I just wanted to give you the two ways above to ponder and digest. If they hit home for you, take a step or two this week to make shift in a different direction. Take a path that is clear of obstacles. Get out of your own way!

Week Twenty Four

The Real Secret

If you've been following me online and in life you've probably noticed that I always make a sincere effort to keep things positive. You may have also noticed how I spend a lot of time doing things that I truly enjoy and believe in. The truth of the matter is that I really love my life. Do you want to know the secret to my joy? The answer is simple...I've never stopped believing in miracles. I've never stopped believing in the impossible. It's that amazing gift that children have that adults often leave behind...after all these years, I've kept mine.

Lately, I've been reveling all up in that gift. I feel like a pre-pubescent pre-teen without the peer pressure and pimples. I possess a renewed spirit of joy and zest for life...not afraid to try new things and never too busy to make time for play.

If you have young children, nieces or nephews, or students you know that one of their main goals is to be entertained at all times. Whenever I plan to spend time with my seven year old nephew, Lil' Ron, I ask him what he'd like to do. His answer is always consistent. "I want to go to the toy store." He is focused on that goal. His answer never changes.

When I'm just coming over for a visit he is certain that I came for a specific reason…not to spend time with my brother or my mother, or to just get away from the city and relax at their place…No. He is confident that I came to visit solely to play with him. He knows what he wants. He knows what brings him joy. He pursues it relentlessly….and guess what? We almost always give in and let him have his way!

Imagine if we all applied that childlike passion to that thing that we love…toward our purpose. Imagine yourself truly believing in miracles and the impossible when it comes to that business that you run or have always wanted to start. Imagine yourself relentlessly pursuing that project, that goal, your education or your ministry. There are several lessons to be learned here…

Know Where You Want to Go

If you called my nephew right this moment and asked him where he wanted to go, I guarantee that he'd say, "the toy store". Know where it is that you want to go. Have a clear vision, remain focused on it and never give up on that until you get it. Be confident, consistent and unafraid to let those people, who want to help you get there, know how they can help.

Know What You Want to Do

As I've mentioned before, one of my favorite quotes says, "If you don't stand for something, you'll fall for anything." This is what often happens when we don't know what we want to do. It's perfectly fine to try out many things, but eventually we must make up our mind about what it is that we want to do. If we flip flop all of the time, or spread ourselves too thin, nothing will get the attention that it deserves. Now that you've identified where you want to go, make sure you know what you want to do to get there.

Know What You Love

As life happens, we have a tendency to forget or abandon what we love. I also often see people get so wrapped up in the lives of the people that they care for that they take on the things that that person loves as their own. I remember times in life where I've had to stop and say "Wait a minute, what's my favorite color? What's my favorite food? What do I enjoy doing? What do I love?" When we know what we love, we often make it a priority to do what we have to in order to keep that person, place or thing at the forefront of our lives. Once we do that, joy follows.

Know What You've Got

This one may seem a little shallow compared to the others, but trust me…it's the stone cold truth. Know what you've got…and work it! My nephew knows that he is super cute. He has the look, the squeaky little voice, the sense of humor, and the personality; and you better believe that he uses every bit of it to his advantage. He knows what makes us laugh or smile. He pays attention to what makes us react. He takes note of the things that don't work and he stops doing them. Take a moment to take inventory of what you've got. It may be a natural charm, a heartwarming smile, quick wit, creativity or a knack for fashion…whatever the case may be…Know it…Own it…and Work it!

Once you've identified all of these things, use them to pursue your goals relentlessly! Think back and tap into your inner child. When you've done that, let your imagination, creativity, passion for play and fearlessness guide you on the path to joy and the realization of your dreams.

Week Twenty Five

The Passenger's Seat

I often take long road trips to literary events or to visit book clubs in other cities around the United States, so it may come as a surprise to you that I AM NOT a big fan of driving. As the hours go by I find myself saying, "I really wish that I was in the passenger seat."

When it comes to life, work and relationships we often try to dictate and control our destiny. This may just sound like a person is being ambitious or a go-getter, but is it actually a lack of faith? We always say that people should "make it happen" but in doing that are we short changing the true possibilities of what we could have if we allowed ourselves to be led?

Think about a sports team. Every team has a captain. In order to be a captain one must be a strong leader...BUT every captain has a coach.

Don't get me wrong...it is great to be driven....but that has a dual meaning. Think about it. If you are a driven person then that means that you set goals, get things done, have a vision, and you are a go getter...BUT if you are driven, or being driven...then that means there is a driver. So once again, you are in the passenger's seat.

Now let's look at it in terms of love and relationships…I may get a little personal or controversial here depending on your view point or situation but keep in mind that these are just my thoughts and opinions.

I'm all about girl power and being an independent woman and everything, but there is nothing like getting all dolled up and having a man pick me up for a date. When I have to pick up a man, all of the time, I find myself feeling cheated or frustrated. I understand that everyone falls upon hard times, and not everyone chooses to have a car, but that is another one of those times where I find myself saying, "I just want to be in the passenger's seat."

So you see, the passenger's seat is not at all a bad thing, it is actually a metaphor for so much more.

In a marriage it symbolizes how a man should be able to lead his wife and family. In business and life it represents how although we should still put in the work, we should exercise our faith, let go of the wheel and trust that God has the power to lead us farther than we can ever take ourselves.

I still have so much more to say on this subject, but for now…let that marinate, then let go and let yourself be led by faith and by the One that is far more qualified and capable than you to steer your life in the right direction…Get in the passenger's seat.

Week Twenty Six

Your Gift Will Make Room for You

"A man's gift makes room for him and brings him before great
men."
–Proverbs 18:16

Take a moment to think about that thing that you are certain is
your God-given gift.

Have you identified it? Is it speaking? Writing? Cooking?
Advocating for those that cannot advocate for themselves?
Educating the masses about a particular issue that needs increased
awareness? Now ask yourself, are you using that gift?

Our gifts are not even about us, they actually have the purpose
of blessing others, but God is really generous because when we are
operating in our gifts we experience a feeling of true bliss. Think
about it. Think about the feelings and sensations that you have
when you are doing what you know that you have been called to
do.

Author, Mihaly Csikszentmihalyi, describes this as a concept called "Flow" which is defined as "an experience involving heightened states of awareness, confidence, and performance; total engagement—you lose yourself in an activity." This happens because we are engaging in something that taps into our intrinsic motivation which means that we don't need any external stimulus or reward in order to do this thing. If no one ever told us that we were doing a great job, if no one ever gave us a grade of A, if we never got paid, we could still wake up and do this thing every morning for the rest of our lives and it would bring us joy. So we experience just as much of a benefit, if not more, than those whose lives we are making a difference in.

If the benefits of our gifts are so vast...then why aren't more people using them? I'd say that the number one reason is fear. This is interesting though, because a lot of us say that we have faith...but faith and fear cannot co-exist. There has to be one or the other. We make excuse after excuse as to why we can't do what we know we are supposed to be doing right now. Money, time, our families...the list goes on and on. But did you know that your gift will make room for you? That in itself should be motivation enough to take the leap, but to even further support that, your gift will also give you access to the great. Let me break that down in terms of my experience...

One day it became crystal clear to me that my gift was to encourage others and help them to realize their dreams using my writing and speaking. As soon as I fully immersed myself in that gift, door after door began to open. It is to the point where it feels as if my path is clear and barrier free…I don't even have to knock anymore because people of high esteem ("The great") are waiting at the open doors saying, "Hey Monica…come on in!" I am at a point where I have to turn down opportunities because I can only do so much at one time. I'm not trying to brag, but do you know that I have never truly had to look for a job? There was really only one time.

When I graduated from graduate school at the University of Michigan with a resume full of credentials and experience, I couldn't seem to find a "job" to save my life. It was at that time that I finally sat down to write my first book. It was a blessing in disguise because if I'd had a job lined up, I never would have sat down to begin putting in the work to prepare to share my gift with the world. Do you see how God works? Every form of income that I have received since then has come in the form of a job, contract, or opportunity that someone specifically sought me out for and offered to me.

You may still not be convinced because you think you don't have the time. You might be working toward a certain goal that is time specific and you think that stopping what you are doing to operate in your gift may get in the way. Well, let me tell you, based on my experience, that if you truly have faith, like you say you do, trust that not only will your gift make a way for you but it will also expedite matters.

As you can see, I could talk about this forever, but I am going to stop here to let what I've said marinate. My challenge to you is to stop trying to dictate everything in your life, get in the passenger's seat and let God and your gift lead you. Then sit back and watch how it will make room for you and put you in the presence of the great!

"A gift opens doors; it gives access to the great." –Proverbs 18:16

Week Twenty Seven

Year of Repair

What is broken in your life? Is it a relationship with a family member, friend or significant other? Is it your credit or financial situation? Is it your health? Is it your education? Is it you? Take a quick diagnostic check or assessment of your life as it is right now and determine what is in need of repair. If you find that there is more than one thing, prioritize them and zero in on that one thing that is at the top of the list.

This year I came to realize that the area where I was the most broken was financial literacy. And isn't it ironic that the root word of broken is "broke". Being "broke" is no more than a mindset or a pattern or behavior that can indeed be broken in a positive way.

In an attempt to fix this area with which I had always been challenged I have officially decided to declare this my "Year of Repair" with a focus on financial literacy. Surprisingly, I have found that as I improve my financial situation through education, awareness and consistent practice of a specific set of action steps, that my self-esteem and confidence have increased and my stress level has decreased. This has, in turn, freed up my time and energy to align and balance all of the other areas in my life that are in need of repair as well.

If you've been reading one chapter a week, you are now approaching the middle of your year of being committed to self-improvement, so now is a good time to reflect upon and reassess the goals that you set for yourself at the beginning of the year. Many of our goals probably spoke directly to the things in our lives that are in need of repair. I just stopped writing this to flip back in my journal to see what my goals were and I realize that I have accomplished four of the eight that I set for myself. I also realize that half of my goals were financial.

This week I challenge you to devote some time to reflecting on where you are in your life, assessing what the challenges or broken pieces are, and begin to plan for how you want to move forward during the second half of your year. Don't overwhelm yourself with several projects, simply focus on one thing that you want to repair and go from there.

Here are a few tips to get you started…

Don't Be Afraid to Ask for Help

There is probably a friend or colleague right within your grasp that is strong in the area in which you are weak.

Never Stop Learning

Study books, magazines, or even documentaries or movies that address the area in which you are broken and striving to repair.

Be Honest With Yourself

A lot of times it's hard to admit areas where we fall short of even our own expectations. Don't be afraid to admit your mistakes and take the first small step to changing your life for the better.

Happy Year of Repair!

Week Twenty Eight

Get Your Life in Order

I've come to know that the state of my physical space is often a pretty accurate representation of my mental and or emotional state. If my car and my loft are junky, then so is my mind. When I'm off balance, overwhelmed, stressed, or just trying to do too much, all of the things around me become a clear sign that it's time to slow down and pull things back together. I usually don't stop to "clean up" until things slow down naturally, but yesterday I began to think...What if we can reverse the effects by flipping the process?

It all boils down to being proactive. What if I began by stopping to take time up front to clean and organize my life? Would that then lend itself to a more clear and organized mind and emotional state?

I decided that I'd give that a try this week. So last night I cleaned up my loft and created a few posters to guide me through the week, the month, and the rest of the year. Take a moment to think about this…What are some practices that we could put into place to make our lives run more smoothly? Here are a few of my suggestions…

Finances

Create a poster of monthly expenses, (also list due dates and amounts) post them on the wall where you have to look at them every day, and cross them off as you pay them off.

Long Term Planning

Create a poster that is a grid of the next six months with blank columns under each month. Write major goals out individually on Post It™ (sticky) notes. Place the goals in the columns under the months in which you hope to accomplish the goals. If life happens and you don't meet one by the due date that you'd planned for, simply move it over to the next month.

Daily Duties

Create a poster similar to the Long Term Planning Poster described above. Instead of months as the column titles, list important components of your life. For me that includes the names of the different companies that I run or consult for, shopping, friends, family and personal. List what needs to be done under each category and cross them off as you accomplish them.

These visual representations of the things that need to be organized and maintained in your life help to keep you on track. Being able to cross them off and see that they have been completed gives you a real sense of accomplishment and progress.

You may not adopt any of these techniques, and I don't encourage you to, if you feel that they won't work for you...BUT this week I will challenge you to come up with one process that will help you to get your life in order, thus improving your mental health and productivity. Engineer yourself for success by beginning with something small and manageable that you know you will stick to. Once you put your new practice into place, sit back and watch how much more smoothly your life will run.

Week Twenty Nine

Under Book and Over Look

Lately I've been exploring meditation in an attempt to quiet my ever racing mind. I've also heard that prayer is you talking to God and meditation is you sitting back quietly to listen for His response. So now, instead of rambling on my long prayers and going about my day immediately after, I've tacked on some meditation time at the end of each prayer to listen to what God has to say back to me.

One day last week I set aside some very intentional quiet time to really get deep into the prayer and meditation. In so many words, the response that I got during my meditation was, "You're doing too much." This made so much sense because I've come to realize that I tend to over book myself. This doesn't mean that I'm scheduling things at the same time, but I'm not really giving myself time to thoroughly breathe, reflect, and rest in between appointments and engagements.

I've come to learn that just because a block of time is not filled on your calendar or in your day planner; it doesn't mean that it's really available. I've had days where I schedule appointments, book signings, meetings and calls back to back to back just because the space is free on my calendar. What I don't account for is transitions, down time, travel time and the fact that I am not a robot and that I might just get tired, somewhere along the way, like humans often do.

When I was given the message that I was doing too much, an example was also revealed to me. At the time I was at a point where my business travel was beginning to slow down a bit, so I'd decided that I was going to commit to thirty days of focus to tie up a lot of loose ends in my life. God was like, "Why does it have to be thirty days? Why can't you just start by committing to like two days and see how that goes?" Again, this made so much sense for me because I definitely have a tendency to make grand plans, then I find myself either overwhelmed by them or disappointed with myself because I've abandoned them.

Another area where I tend to do too much is within my thoughts. I have formed a nasty little habit of sweating the small stuff, instead of focusing on the big picture. Sometimes we all stress ourselves out by thinking about, paying attention to and entertaining some of the most trivial things. Let's use a dating situation as a common example of this...

A man and a woman are dating. The woman spends a lot of time and energy paying attention to all of the other young ladies that are attracted to or interested in her man. She overlooks the fact that she gets all of his time, attention and affection, and focuses on all of these women that are making comments on his Facebook page or following him on Twitter. Instead of focusing on the positive big picture, she is zeroed in on the insignificant small picture. My advice to her would be, "If you are the quarterback, why in the world are you worried about who's on the bench?"

Do you see where I'm going with this?

This week I challenge you to UNDER book yourself for a change and OVER book the small stuff that doesn't even matter in the larger scheme of things. As your personal guinea pig for positive change, I can assure you that your life will begin to improve instantly.

Week Thirty

TAG! You're IT!

Think of the game called Tag that we used to play when we were children. You run for your life from the person that's "It" like getting caught by them is the worst thing in the world...the worst thing that could possibly happen. We don't stop to think about what happens when we get caught. The reality is that the outcome is not that bad at all. When you get caught, you become "It" and now you have the power.

Now think about how this parallels with our lives. We often run from our problems, namely bill collectors or facing hard choices and decisions that we must make.

Take your power back! Stop running from your fears and problems; turn around and start chasing and pursuing them. I've been doing this for the first half of this year and it's not only been far less painful than I thought it would be, but it's actually been quite liberating. Set up payment arrangements with those bill collectors and see if there are opportunities for settlements where you square away what you owe by paying a smaller lump sum. Talk to people about how you feel. Make those hard decisions and stick to them. When you face your problems and your fears head on, they are nowhere near as frightening as they seemed when you were running and hiding.

It's time to take responsibility for the fact that our fears are often our own fault. Yes, bill collectors may be a little rude and snippy at times, but hey, they're just doing their job. We are the ones that did not keep our word, or pay our bill, or bought something we knew we really couldn't afford.

Fear only has the power that you give it. Just like a car, it can't go anywhere or do anything unless you give it the fuel.

This week I challenge you to stop running; turn around and chase your fear right back. These days, as I work diligently to repair my credit; the bill collectors are my friends, not my enemies. I call them regularly to see what type of deals I can work out with them and I even go as far as joking with them. I keep it pleasant and positive and they often have no other choice but to reciprocate those delightful behaviors.

What are you running from?

Take your power back TODAY....TAG! You're IT!

Week Thirty One

Help IS the Way

There's a song that goes, "Hold on, Help is on the way!" If you have faith, you know that this is a statement that is very true, but what we usually fail to even consider is that help IS THE WAY to speed up the process.

We often believe that we've exhausted every option when it comes to trying to improve a situation, solve a problem, or reach a goal in our lives. There's one secret key that we always forget about. That secret key is asking how we can be of assistance to someone else. The saying "Give to Get" doesn't just apply to money. We can give our time, wisdom, experience or advice to those in need. Keep in mind that when I say "those in need" I don't just mean the "needy." Successful people are often the people that need the most help; there is a lot to be learned and gained just from being in their presence. Let's cut right to the chase and look at a few concrete examples of how helping others gives you a high return on the investment of your time…

Years ago I worked at an after school program where the teens would often ask about employment opportunities. I'd built a relationship with them, so they trusted me when I told them that there weren't currently any opportunities, but they should volunteer in the meantime. Sure enough, a few months we were awarded grant money to pay teen staff and since those particular young people had been diligently volunteering, they were first in line to get hired. How can you apply this example to your life? Are you seeking employment? You're never too young or too old to be an intern or a volunteer and you can work your way up. Most major executives started out this way.

Now let's take a look at my writing career. In college I studied elementary education and then social work. I'd never taken a writing class, but I knew that I wanted to write and publish a book. As soon as I moved back to Detroit, I immediately began volunteering for the Motown Writers Network. I basically latched myself on to the founder, Sylvia Hubbard, and volunteered to help her in any way that I could. Over ten years and five books later, anytime she comes across an awesome opportunity for a book signing, speaking engagement, publishing opportunity or whatever, I am one of the first people that she calls. So, as if all of the valuable information that I've learned by helping her over the years wasn't reward enough, I also get these ongoing perks that continue to help me grow my business and my brand. If it wasn't for my giving of my time, there is NO way that I'd be as far along as I am today. Is there an industry that you would like to learn more about? If you volunteer for some of that industry's major events you can forgo the registration costs but still learn all of the valuable information while you are helping.

When some people hear the concept of doing something for free it sounds foreign to them or even absurd, but what they miss is that when you give, you benefit as much or more than the person that you are helping.

Think about it like this. Let's say you charge $30 per hour for consulting and you help someone with what they are dealing with for two hours. Your profit will end at that $60 if you even get the contract. Now if you volunteer to help someone, the rewards and benefits you get are often infinite. It may lead to referrals for more contracts, paid speaking engagements, or free access to things that you might have otherwise had to pay for equaling thousands in profit or money saved. Volunteering just keeps on giving in ways that hold far more value than that mere $60. Now I'm not suggesting that you not know your worth and charge accordingly for it, I'm just making sure that you are aware of the powerful impact and benefit of simply offering your free gift of help.

This week I challenge you to reach out and help someone. Simply ask, "How can I help or support you?" Pick someone who has successfully achieved some of the goals that you hope to achieve. Think Big! Target the top five people that you have been watching and hoping to someday accomplish what they have. I'll be tackling this challenge by trying to meet a millionaire mentor. In the midst of my helping them, I can pick their brain to see how they got to where I want to be.

After you've done all you can, try a new approach. Help IS the way.

Week Thirty Two

Rehab

The word rehabilitation is often given a bad reputation. It is associated with the process by which someone goes through detox, therapy and behavior modification to help them recover from an addiction to drugs or alcohol. Very rarely do we look at it as the positive thing that it is meant to be. If we looked at the bright side of it, we would see that it is a way for people to restore and rebuild their lives.

Let's look at it in terms of real estate. When you buy an investment property it may be distressed or need repair. Investing in the rehabilitation that the house needs will substantially increase its value. Even something as simple as painting the walls can make the property worth more than you acquired it for, thus making it more marketable and in higher demand once you present it to the world.

I want you to think of yourself or your life as that house. What projects need to be done to increase your value? What investment do you need to make in yourself to increase your worth? Perhaps you need to strengthen or reinforce your foundation by continuing your academic or financial education. Or maybe the improvements are structural in that you need to commit or re-commit to fitness. You might need new windows, representing your vision or the way that you look at things.

Are you looking at life from a point of view that is broken or damaged? A new storm door represents security...do you need to work on being more secure in who you are, especially in the face of a storm or adversity. Whether the changes are large or small they can all increase your net worth in a major way.

This week I challenge you to do your due diligence and conduct a thorough inspection of yourself. Make a list of the projects that need attention, in order of priority, and begin your process of rehabilitation with the most pressing one. In the end you will find yourself in a better place with more confidence and self-assurance because you put in the work needed to increase your value and your worth.

Let the rehabilitation begin!

Week Thirty Three

Increase Your Peace

My Mother and I had a really good conversation the other day. During the discussion she said that as a person gets older, their life should become more peaceful, and they should have far more grace when it comes to the way in which they handle situations. It may seem that the opposite is the case with the way reality TV glorifies grown folks fighting, but it still rings true that as your age increases, so should your peace and grace.

This year I've made an intentional effort to improve the quality of my life. Just last week I was sitting in my loft and I thought to myself, "My life is really peaceful. I am happy." There was a time in the past where I wouldn't have been honestly able to say that.

There were certain things in my life that I had to change, replace, add or take away on my personal journey to peace and grace. The first step was being brutally honest…with me.

I know that I do well under pressure, which is fine every now and then, but overall I had to replace procrastination with planning. My lack of advanced planning often led me to be reactive to situations, so I had to replace that with being proactive. Being reactive often came with a lot of emotion. I had to replace the emotion with logic. Emotion usually leads to drama, so once I got rid of that, the drama decreased and I became ready to increase my peace. Increased peace leads to grace. When you are peaceful and happy, you handle situations far more gracefully.

I was reading a book by one of my favorite authors, Robert T. Kyosaki, the other day and he said that in order for him to make meaningful and lasting change, certain parts of him had to die. For example, in order for him to be rich…the poor man in him had to die. In order for him to be healthy, the fat and lazy man in him had to die…

What part of us needs to die, so that the new and improved version can be born?

This week I challenge you to think about the habits and behaviors in your life that you can replace, change or eliminate in order to increase your peace and grace. Take it one day at a time…and take it from me, the end result is well worth the work.

Week Thirty Four

Simplify Your Life to Live

"Why are you ALWAYS in such a rush?" These words stopped me in my tracks and made me ask myself the same question. My nephew said this to me one Friday when I breezed back into town after being gone for a week and only stopped by momentarily to give him a hug and a kiss on the cheek. He had other plans. He wanted me to sit and play with him and his super hero action figures. So instead of rushing out of the door to run errands, keep appointments, and squeeze in everything that I could before leaving town again on Sunday...I sat down with him and just played.

It was interesting that he said this to me because the previous week I facilitated a training exercise where I asked the participants to talk about their goals; two of the participants said that their goal was to simplify their life. This stood out to me because usually people have complex personal or professional goals that include losing weight, starting a business, obtaining a degree or writing a book. I realized that for me, simplifying my life might have been just as challenging as any of those other goals.

Sometimes, when we are good at something, it is our natural tendency to feel like that is what we are supposed to be doing and we pour all of our energy into it. I've learned the hard way that just because you excel at something, it doesn't mean that you are supposed to be doing that thing.

There was a point in my life, where I gave time to everything that I was good at…acting, dancing, modeling, teaching, community work and youth work. I figured that since all of the things that I was engaged in were positive, then there was no problem with me doing them all. What I came to learn was that stress comes in all forms, not just from negative things or when things are not going your way. You can just as easily become stressed out from doing a whole lot of positive things too.

There have been several instances where I took something that I loved, and gave it so much of myself, that I ended up turning myself off to it altogether. I'll give you an example. I love to dance. Instead of just dancing like no one was watching because it brings me joy, I ended up dancing professionally, and then teaching dance. My joy became work, and I ended up retiring from it. Being a dance teacher was great, but that's not what I really wanted. I simply wanted to dance. Even though I may have exposed my students to new and wonderful experiences, I ruined it for myself.

I realized that this is a pattern for me. I take something that I love, and end up taking a road that I may not have been meant to take. The problem with this is that when we overdo anything, we end up burning ourselves out. It's just like food, if you cook it too long, or at too high of a temperature, it burns.

Essentially, it's all about finding a balance. It's great to give your all to what you believe in, but don't spread yourself too thin. I've always had a desire in my heart to change the world, so I tend to try to do fifty million different things to accomplish that goal. Eventually I find myself tired and overwhelmed. If I'm feeling that way, what good am I to the people that I hope to encourage?

My point: Keep it simple. At the end of the day, that's all that matters anyway…the simple things. If you find yourself feeling stressed and overwhelmed more than you find yourself at peace, it may be time to scale back your life. Someone said, "Maybe you need to clear some things off of your plate." My response was, "Maybe I need to get a smaller plate!"

This week I challenge you to identify one to three things that you can eliminate from your schedule that will help to simplify your life, thus reducing your stress and anxiety. It may also be a matter of adding something to your schedule, like budgeting your money to make things flow more smoothly for you in the long run, or beginning a workout, such as cardio kickboxing, that will help you to reduce stress.

Once you've done this, simply sit back and savor the simple things that truly matter. Play with your children before you look up one day and realize that they are all grown up. Watch the sun rise or set. Color in a coloring book. Watch a silly movie. Read a good book. Talk to a friend on the phone about nothing of importance. Or do what seems to be the most challenging thing of all for most of us busy over-achievers…simply sit down. These are the things that make life worth living. Simplify your life and begin to live.

Week Thirty Five

Where is Your Focus?

Motivational speakers, teachers, business professionals and the like spend a lot of time talking about how important it is to focus. This is true; however, more time might need to be spent talking about what we are focusing on. It is implied that we focus on the positive, but perhaps it needs to be more clearly stated. We have a natural tendency to shift most, or all, of our focus to negative things, such as what we don't have or what is wrong in our lives.

We always talk about how we can't wait to get more money, a better job, a bigger house and so on, but once we get those things are we truly happy with them?

I had to catch myself recently. I am living my dream life right now, but every now and then I find myself slipping into focusing on the negative side of things. I was talking with a friend about how I struggle with anxiety when I travel because I miss my family and friends and I feel like I'm missing out on something back at home.

My friend had to snap me back to reality by saying, "You have a life that most people only dream of. Why are you complaining?" I had to stop and say, "You know what, you're right!" I had to place my focus on the fact that I love what I do. My work affords me the opportunity to travel all over the world; as a result, I am able to live comfortably and help my loved ones.

This week I encourage you to examine the subject of your focus. You might be an extremely focused person but, the question is, "Are you focusing on the right things?" Shift your focus from what is wrong and lacking in your life to more positive matters such as the things that are going well and your vision for personal and professional growth.

Week Thirty Six

Take a Chance on Life

Sometimes we get so caught up in what we don't want to happen that we forget to accept and embrace what we do want. This usually happens in two major areas: our work and our love life.

Let's take a look at our work first. We may be at a job that makes us completely miserable, but we find every excuse under the sun as to why we can't leave, when just the fact of being miserable alone is reason enough. The main thing we say is that we don't want to lose the benefits. What will we do if we get sick? What will we do if we get into a car accident? Well the first thing that I learned about working in a toxic environment is that I never got sick until I started working there, so yes, if you continue to work in an unhealthy environment, you just may need to go to the doctor.

I also learned that in a lot of cases, benefits were not the magic answer. I learned that the hard way, when my benefits didn't cover the services that the dentist convinced me needed to be done before I could get a basic check-up and cleaning. As for the car accident, God forbid, if you even have to get treated, then you'll just have to pay off your bill in installments, just like you do with many other bills that aren't covered by your health insurance benefits.

Sometimes when we hold on to something like a miserable job, we don't allow room for the new amazing job, investment opportunity, or new business venture to come into our lives. We are so fixated on our circumstance that we can't see the other awesome possibilities that are all around us. I took on a mantra a couple of years ago and I constantly have to remind myself of it. It says, "Stop complaining and do something about it. If you're not going to do anything to make the situation better, then shut up!"

The same is often the case with love. We say we want this wonderful, honest, good looking, and hardworking mate, but when we meet that person, we are suddenly scared. We are scared to be hurt or disappointed or we begin to feel like it must be too good to be true.

Don't you know that you will get what you ask for if you believe that you will receive it? But keep in mind that this goes both ways. You may be with that person now, or you may still be waiting. If you are waiting, prepare yourself now to be ready for what you asked for. If you've never had a healthy relationship, it will certainly take some getting used to. If you have a great relationship, don't sabotage it by not believing that you deserve it, or waiting for something to go wrong. Savor every moment and receive the blessing that you've been praying and asking for.

This week I challenge you to take a look at your work and love life and ask yourself if you are giving both a fair shot. Will you complain or sabotage? Or will you make the necessary changes and embrace the goodness? Take a chance on life. Take a chance on love. Take a chance on happiness.

Week Thirty Seven

What Are You Chasing?

Take a moment to inventory how you spend your time. Most likely you spend some, if not the majority of your time going after something. That thing may be money, a mate, or a goal. Having your sights set on something to strive toward can be a great thing. The question is: are you going after the best thing for you?

When it comes to life, love and even success, there is something about the chase that is very exciting. We like to go after what's challenging, what we are told we can't have, or what may seem unattainable. In many instances this is a good thing, but is what you are chasing, what you are supposed to have?

ARE YOU MISSING SOMETHING THAT YOU ARE SUPPOSED TO GET BY CHASING SOMETHING THAT YOU ARE NOT SUPPOSED TO HAVE?

We have a tendency, often subconsciously, to try to manipulate and control our lives. We see something we want and then we create every reason that we can as to why it is what we are supposed to have. As a result, we often find ourselves in situations that may not be healthy for us. So it's important to take time to think through our decisions and our choices to make sure that in trying to pursue what we want, we are not missing out on what we are supposed to have.

This week I challenge you to analyze your current circumstance. What are you chasing? Does it want to be caught? If you stop chasing it, will it chase you? When it's something that you're supposed to have, it will most likely come when you stop looking. Make room for your blessings by opening up your mind and your heart to receive them. Sometimes that means just being still and waiting faithfully and patiently. Take a break from the chase so that you can get what you are supposed to have.

Week Thirty Eight

Is Your Thinking Stinking?

One day at church the pastor said that when you are going through hell…the only way that hell could have gotten inside of you, or your home, is through your mind. His words were exactly what I needed to hear because I'd been dealing with negative thoughts all that week to the point where I was losing sleep. As much as I motivate and encourage others, I was slowly being taken out by entertaining negative thinking.

It all boils down to fear and we know that fear and faith can't co-exist. I don't mean to recap his whole sermon, but he was so on point that I'd be doing you an injustice if I didn't share. The other profound point that he made had to do with faith. He said that there are three things that need to be in place in order for faith to be faith: 1.) Believe it. 2.) Speak it. 3.) Act on it.

Believe It

See yourself in the future. Whatever it is that you want to happen…you must believe that it will. Visualize it. Picture it. Draw it if you have to. Think of it as already being yours.

Speak It

We often underestimate the power of our words. You will begin to see what you say, so choose your words wisely and keep them positive.

Act on It

We can believe it and speak it all day, but if we don't act on it, we might as well go right back to living in fear or allowing hell into our home and into our mind. Another important point that the pastor made is that sometimes the corresponding action to the faith is to "shut up and wait." What are the proper actions that will go along with what you believe for?

I'm usually extremely positive, but that particular week I was all out of character. I had to check myself. It all came down to changing my thinking. Now, when negative thoughts try to enter my mind, I picture myself swatting them away with a tennis racket. That may seem silly, but hey, it works for me so I encourage you to do what works for you.

This week, I challenge you to check yourself to make sure that you aren't allowing negativity, fear, self-doubt or any other stinking thinking to seep into your subconscious. Remember, the only way that hell can enter your life is through your thoughts AND the only way that hell can exit your life...is through your thoughts.

Week Thirty Nine

Ask for What You're Worth

When I travel to do consulting or speaking engagements, the clients generally cover travel expenses. I am often given the option to choose my flight preferences. For those of you that travel frequently, you know that connecting flights can be a nightmare. If your first flight is delayed, then it may make you miss your second flight. Another headache is when you end up in airports and on planes all day because your layover in between flights is so long. Either way, it makes for a stressful and draining day of travel, which often takes away from the energy needed for the performance that you plan to give when you speak, teach or train. Needless to say, my preference is for non-stop flights.

As I was looking through flights for an upcoming engagement I realized that most of them had connections. I also noticed that the ones with the layovers were considerably more affordable than the ones that were non-stop flights on my airline of choice.

This time I decided to try something a little different. Instead of feeling bad for choosing a more expensive flight, or trying to save the company money by selecting the cheapest flight, or even sending my top three choices…I simply sent my first choice and left it at that.

As I waited for the response I began searching for my second and third choice because I felt that surely they wouldn't honor my first request. It was too expensive. I got prepared to accept my fate of having to take a cheaper flight even though all of the departure and arrival times were either ridiculously late or painfully early.

In the midst of my melancholy search I received a response. It was the confirmation for my first choice flight! It was a non-stop flight on my desired airline. The client booked it without a question or a concern. They saw the value in my services thus matching the quality that they know I will deliver with the accommodations that they arranged for me. It made me realize that 'affordable' and 'expensive' are all about perspective. If we want something different for ourselves, we must think differently about ourselves. If I thought of myself as priceless, then I wouldn't have thought of that flight as being too expensive.

The lesson in all of this is two-fold. The first is that you must know your worth. If you expect and accept less, then that's exactly what you will get…less than what you are worth. Look at it like this…if someone said, "I want to give you some money." And your response was, "You can give me $5 or $500 or $5000." Which one do you think they would choose? Most people would probably go with $5 since you gave them that option. Don't low ball yourself - start high because you are worth it. If negotiations are necessary then so be it, but don't settle for less than what you are worth. When you ask for less it may cause those who you are communicating with to believe that you are not qualified or confident when it comes to your ability to execute the task.

The second lesson is that you must ask for exactly what you want. You'd be surprised at how often you actually get it. We have not because we ask not. A more common occurrence is that we have not, because we ask for less than what we truly want or are worth.

This week I challenge you to ask for what you want. The worst thing that can happen is that someone can tell you "no"...they can't kill you. If you don't know your worth, then perhaps you should take out some time to learn about it. Once you know your worth, adjust accordingly.

Week Forty

How Do You Talk About YOU?

How do you talk about you? If you hear something so often for so long you start to believe it. Your own voice, whether it's speaking internally or out loud is the one that you hear the most. Since you have committed to this journey of clearing out old things in your life and bringing in new things, you may want to remodel how you speak about and to yourself.

I've lost count of how many times I've heard people say, "I feel so ugly" or "I'm fat". I might as well just start responding to them by saying, "You sure are." What we speak seeps into our subconscious and subliminally hypnotizes us into believing what we are saying. As result we end up becoming those things…even if it is only in our own mind. No matter what others see, when we look in the mirror, we only see what we've spoken ourselves into being.

Even more detrimental than negative self-talk that focuses on physical appearance is when people defeat themselves, before they even try, by speaking negatively about their ability.

For years I taught dance to young people and I got to a point where I had to ban the words "can't" and "don't" from my classroom. I told my students that those were curse words. They took it so seriously that when a new student came and said one of those words, or an existing student slipped up, there would be a collective "Oooooooooh!" It was that sound we make when someone is about to get in trouble.

I had those children convinced that those were two more four-letter words to add to the list of profanities that they weren't supposed say. But if you look at the term 'curse word' literally, it is like we are putting a curse on ourselves when we speak so negatively. I would ask those young people, "How do you know what you can't or don't know how to do before you've even tried?"

This week, I challenge you to focus on changing the way that you talk to and about yourself. Out with the old negative self-talk and in with the new positive self-talk or affirmations.

"An affirmation is a positive statement of (positive) belief, and if we can become one-tenth as good at positive self-talk as we are at negative self-talk, we will notice an enormous change."
– Julia Cameron, Author of The Artist's Way

Week Forty One

Everything Happens for a Reason

One Monday morning I was sitting in Detroit Metro Airport after having missed my early morning flight to Rochester, New York. There was once a time where if something like that happened I might have cried or been frustrated to the point of making myself physically sick. But on that morning I sat there just as calm and cool as a cat because of something my Mother always told me... "Everything happens for a reason."

I called my Mom to let her know that I'd missed my flight and after about thirty-seven seconds of sympathy she said, "What happened to last week's Monday Morning Motivation? Why didn't I get it? Did this new anti-virus software remove it from my computer?"

I had to smile. I didn't send out a Monday Morning Motivation the week before because of the holiday and it wasn't looking like I was going to be able to send one out on that day either because of the early travel and business that I needed to prepare for. Well wouldn't you know; I guess God had different plans for me that day. Perhaps I missed that flight just so I could get that message out to someone that needed to hear it.

I strongly believe that when something is placed on your heart, you must get it out, because you never know who's watching and who needs to hear, feel or see your message. Just a few days ago I got a message from a young lady out of the blue. She wanted to let me know that she'd read my first book, "The Ups and Downs of Being Round" and that it inspired her to lose over 100 pounds!

I was so excited to be able to touch, and in some ways save, a person's life in such a way. It speaks to a motivational message that I wrote in the past based upon a quote by a dear friend. In short, when we don't operate in our gifts, people could be dying. I know that sounds harsh, but most of us know what we are supposed to be doing, and when we do operate in that purpose, we save lives.

Sometimes when seemingly bad things happen, we get angry or upset, but we must keep in mind that everything happens for a reason. Whatever has transpired may have saved us from something worse or it may be preparing us for something greater. I wasn't supposed to be on that flight that morning. If I was, I would have been on it. I trust that it happened for a very specific reason. When something happens to you that seems like it's the worst thing in the world, take a deep breath and know that there is a greater purpose behind it.

As I was sitting there at the airport wrapping up the writing of this very message, a man that worked there came up to me and asked me how I liked my mini net book computer. I could have had a bad attitude, especially toward the employees of the airline since I missed my flight because the attendant wasn't at the gate ten minutes before departure, then the plane pulled off earlier than scheduled. He and I got to talking about what I do and he just gave me a huge valuable chunk of financial wisdom that I've been praying about. At that point I knew it was official…that day was going to be a great day. No matter what happens, good or bad, know that it is for a reason and a purpose so just smile and keep the faith!

Week Forty Two

What's in Your Backpack?

People often say that when something bad happens, or when you go through something, that you're supposed to put the past behind you and move on. This advice has always seemed to make a lot of sense but now that I think about it, where does all of that past that you're chucking over your shoulder go?

For years, every time I experienced a setback, a failure, a disappointment or the like, I simply tossed it behind me and kept things moving along at a rather brisk pace. Then one day I realized that I just felt heavy. I got to a place where I could not move forward anymore.

In church, on Sunday, the Pastor touched on this subject and he said that back in olden days the punishment for killing a man was that his dead body would be tied to your back. Imagine having to go through life with a heavy, smelly rotting dead person on your back.

That dead person represents the old you. I know that image is rather grotesque so let's liken the dead person or the old you to an oversized and over stuffed backpack.

When you put your failures behind you, you are placing them in an overweight back pack that represents your emotional and psychological baggage. In order to move forward it is necessary to acknowledge or address those things or people that have hurt or harmed you. I've found peace and healing in using those negative situations in my writing, thus helping others while simultaneously freeing myself of the extra baggage.

This week I encourage you to remove that back pack; empty it out. Lay the things that were in it out before you. Deal with them, learn from them, and use them as stepping stones so that you may reach further and higher without the heavy burden.

Week Forty Three

Vision: It's Time for a New Prescription

One weekend I set aside some time to design the loft that I live in to make it more conducive to the creative space that I need to be in to write. I believe that our physical environment has a direct effect, not only on our creativity, but also on our mood and productivity. Many people agree with this belief but everyone has a very different perception of what this looks like.

As a part of my design process, I treated myself to my first, very own, top of the line bed complete with one thousand thread count Egyptian cotton sheets. This may seem like no big deal, but for me it was a major milestone. This was my first time purchasing my very own bed that was not a hand-me-down or some other complicated situation. What does that say about me? For years, I put many of my basic needs on the back burner while trying to cater to the needs of others in an effort to save the world. Well, even super heroes need somewhere comfortable to lay their head at night. The mini moral here is that we won't be of much good to anyone else, if we are not first good to ourselves.

The movers came and one of them felt compelled to tell me, before he even saw my loft that he doesn't think this is a good place to live. He based it upon several reasons, one being that I live across from an adult rehabilitation facility. He went on to support his point by saying that when he walks out of his door, he wants to see something beautiful. He said that when I walk out my door I see killers and criminals.

I defended my space by saying, well what about the view of the river? He said, "Oh, that's not a real view, that building is in the way, and there's an abandoned lot..."

The funny thing is, no matter how much supporting evidence he provided to support his claim, never once did he change my lens or my frame.

If things aren't looking so good in your life, perhaps it's time to change the lens through which you view them. If that doesn't work, then change the frame. The lens is your vision or perception. The frame is your mindset. Your situation can improve as quickly as you can change your mind and your outlook.

Here is how I view my situation. First of all, I live in Detroit...a city that I admire for its resilience...a city that I love...a city that I won't give up on just for the simple fact that so many others already have or want to. Second of all, my vision reaches so high and so far that I see beyond the busy street, beyond the buildings, beyond the vacant lots, straight to the river that is framed by the sky. I look at it as a beautiful glimpse of God's great creation. It is only one piece in His vast collection of living art work.

And finally, I don't look at the men that reside in that adult rehabilitation facility as criminals or killers. I look at them as men with enough courage to take the first step to seek help. They are men who are starting the beginning of the rest of their lives. They are men who are on the cusp of a breakthrough who will go on to share their testimony to touch the lives of others in need.

Perhaps I view the world through rose colored glasses, but my outlook is what motivates me to inspire and encourage others. My positive mindset is what has freed me from the trappings of the mental health issues that plague our community, especially in economic times such as this.

So my friends, perhaps it's time for a new prescription. New lenses, new frames and thus a beautiful start to a new life free from so much heartache and pain.

Week Forty Four

Step Back to Move Forward

Sometimes we can't see a situation for what it is while we are in it. It is not until we take a step back that we are able to truly see the big picture.

Imagine standing with your nose touching the side of a house. All that you might see is a small space of white aluminum siding. Take one step back and a window may come into view. Take another step back and you may see a door. Take a few more steps back and the garden, grass and entire house may come into view. The space that you were initially zoomed in on may have been really clean, or really dirty, but once you stepped back, and took in the full picture, the true case may have been just the opposite.

The same is the case with our relationships and environments. When we are in it, or right up on it, we may not be able to clearly see it for what it truly is. There are two sides to this. We may have the false perception that our situation is better than it truly is, or we may be so focused on where we are that we do not see all of the open doors and windows, greener grass or in essence, the possibilities all around us.

So today look at your jobs, your relationship and your environment from a different angle. Taking a few steps back might symbolize taking some space, time for self, or maybe a vacation. Perhaps the very reason that the situation is so strained is because you are smothering it by not giving it the room, the space or the light that it needs to grow and flourish.

Imagine standing over a plant trying to will it to grow. You'd be blocking the sunlight and neglecting to give it the water that it needs because you are too busy being all up on it. While you are in the midst of your mess, or your make-believe happiness, you have a skewed view. In order to move forward when you're feeling stagnant, stifled, or stuck...take a step back.

Week Forty Five

The Mirror

Ever since I stepped out on faith to pursue writing full time, I have been making a point to attend events and engage in activities that add to my life in a positive way...personal development, if you will. Attending workshops, seminars and expos, reading motivational books, and even meeting with people that I consider to be mentor material, has become a regular part of my schedule for the purpose of keeping me positive, productive, and constantly immersed in the process of growth.

One night, I attended an event called "Ladies Can We Talk." The event was hosted by, motivational speaker and author, Lisa Nichols as a part of her promotional tour for the Chicken Soup for the African American Woman's Soul anthology. I invited my spiritual mentor and went in totally expecting that we would be fed a lecture style motivational speech. To my surprise it was very interactive and all of the participants added value to the experience. There was standing room only because the organizers had anticipated two hundred women, but there were three hundred twenty-six people in attendance, including a few men.

Throughout the evening we had to do several activities with a partner. I felt like I'd been strategically placed with the exact person that I needed to connect with. Before I even knew that this woman was going to be my partner I'd noticed her. I noticed that she was very pretty and well dressed. "Now there is a woman that's got herself together," I thought to myself. During the activities we were told to sit face-to-face and knee-to-knee. It was slightly uncomfortable at first because we were strangers to one another, but the facilitators had warned us in advance that our comfort level would be significantly challenged.

Once we began to share deep truths about ourselves with one another I realized that my reflection had been placed before me. I was looking at my reflection literally and figuratively. This woman's features were very similar to my own, so much so, that if we told people that we were biologically related, no one would protest or give it a second thought.

It was like looking in a mirror that reflected me ten years into the future. This woman was ten years my senior, but was experiencing many of the issues that I was dealing with during that time. This outwardly beautiful and polished woman suffered from the exact same insecurities that I had. Like me, she had gotten into relationships at a very young age and somehow missed the very important developmental stages of autonomy and self-efficacy. That is, knowing and loving one's self.

I feel like I was shown what my life would be like in the future if I continued to neglect to know and love myself. I was shown how my life would be if I rushed into marriage without first engaging in a committed relationship with myself. While I don't think that this woman or her life is bad, I know that it is not where I want to be. This was confirmed for me when she communicated to me that she didn't want to be there either, and it was her life.

We may not always literally hear or see what we need to learn about life and ourselves, but that small voice speaks to us through people and circumstances. I felt so connected to this woman that I had never met in my life before that day. I believe it's safe to say that she experienced the same feeling of connection to me. I also believe that she would give anything to be in the position that I am in, where I still have the chance and the choice to change the course of my life and my thinking while I am still young. I will use the wisdom that she imparted upon me to inform my decisions and behaviors because I owe it to her, and to myself.

So pay attention to those that cross your path because they are placed there for a reason. Perhaps your mirror messenger will answer that burning question that you've always wanted answered. So be still and patient and, in the meantime, surround yourself with positive energy.

Week Forty Six

Morning Routines
That Make Your Day

We often blame people, situations or circumstances for the times when we have a bad day, but what we fail to realize is that no one has the power to ruin our day but us. What we say and do when we wake up determines the direction that our day will take.

I've found that I am far more productive when I have a morning ritual that sets a positive tone for the rest of my day. Many mornings I wake up by 9am at the latest so that I can watch an inspirational television program. During the show I eat a healthy breakfast and after the show I read something that will add value to my life in some way. That entire process takes thirty minutes to an hour and it's my jump start to setting my day in the right direction. Not only do I have the inspiration that I need to keep me going, but I've also started off with a nutritious meal that will increase my energy and metabolism.

Here are a few routines that I recommend to get your day off to the right start. Choose one that works for you, or come up with your own and start tomorrow.

A Daily Affirmation

Memorize or post positive words and say them out loud. My favorite affirmation is, "I am now open to receive." I love this one because a lot of times we say that we want better things in life like money, joy or love...but the truth is that we are not ready or open to receive those things.

A dear friend and colleague of mine overcame a very serious disease. When I asked her how she did it her answer was, "Daily Affirmations".

Meditation and Prayer

Setting aside a specific time for focused meditation and prayer may be the only time of peace and quiet for people who have hectic lives and schedules. Take this time to give thanks for all that you have, and to ask for all that you want or need. Also, use this time to take some deep restorative breaths, because how often do you go through the entire day without taking a deep breath? I know that I've been guilty of this offense, so let's all stop what we are doing right now and take a deep breath....

Ahhhh...Now doesn't that feel good? So make meditation, prayer and deep breathing a part of your day right from the start!

Exercise

Whether it is stretching, Yoga, or a brisk walk or run, some type of movement each morning is a great way to start your day. Believe it or not, it increases your energy throughout the day. I also like the idea that if I get it done in the morning, I am less likely to put it off and end up skipping it all together.

These are just a few ideas, but I encourage you to try something that works for you because ultimately, the tone, energy and flow of your day is up to you, so why not make it positive right from the start.

Week Forty Seven

Don't Wait for the Weight

One morning I almost got discouraged when my weight had increased by five pounds from the previous day's reading, but then I had to catch myself and remember how the scale can be a true set-up. Several factors contribute to the reasons why our weight on the scale may fluctuate from day-to-day and sometimes throughout the day. From my research, I have found that our true weight is the weight that we see first thing in the morning when we wake up after we have used the bathroom. We must also keep in mind that different scales are calibrated differently thus giving us a different reading. Don't pay so much attention to the number. Pay attention to the gain and loss and try to stick with one scale. No matter what actual weight any scale may say, if you lose five pounds, you lose five pounds...just as five pounds of feathers weighs the same as five pounds of bricks.

I came to the conclusion that my weight had increased so rapidly due to two factors. One was that I had not used the bathroom yet as I always do when I wake up in the morning. The other factor was that, the day before, I had consumed far less water and far more sodium than usual, so I was suffering from water retention.

This is another reason why we should not rely solely on the scale as a measure of our progress, because often times the change that we see is a water weight loss or gain, not fat. I like to measure my progress by keeping track of my inches, gauging how my clothes feel, and measuring my body fat percentage. This helps me because I carry weight much differently than most.

When asked to guess my weight, many guess an average forty pounds lighter than what I actually weigh. When I reveal my actual weight to people, they usually don't believe me. When I was hovering around the forty pound lighter weight that they guessed me to be, I began to look too skinny and I had lost all of my womanly curves, thus I have come to the conclusion that the weight that I am right now is the ideal weight for me. I believe that I tend to weigh more because of the fact that muscle weighs more than fat. I have a lot of muscle, primarily in my legs.

I have made the conscious decision to enjoy and love my body as it is in the present. I will continue to work out, eat right, and strive to increase my quality of health and level of fitness, but I will not wait until I reach a certain goal weight to do everything that I want to do. I hear people saying that they want to wait until they shed the pounds to take pictures, put on a swim suit or perform in a show....I used to be the same way. While using things such as this for motivation to become healthier is great, I no longer believe in putting my life on hold. You can try to put life on hold if you want to, but life won't wait for you. Take it from me, I speak from experience.

I've had times where I felt too fat, then I lost sixty-five pounds and I felt too skinny, missing my womanly curves and feeling like I was shaped like a little boy. Now, I look back at pictures and see how beautiful I was at every moment of my life, even when I was at my highest weight of two hundred fourteen pounds....the key is believing it. When you believe that you are beautiful, you exude a confidence that is magnetic.

With all of that said, I will not wait to do a professional photo shoot, I will not wait to wear a two piece swim suit, and I will not wait to do everything I aspire to do. I will not wait for the weight!

Weight may not be your issue, but I'm sure that there is something in your life, such as money or time, that you use as an excuse to stop you from enjoying and experiencing life to the fullest. This week I challenge you to stop waiting for that thing and take action.

Week Forty Eight

Personal Development
Has a High ROI

As we settle into each new season, it makes me think about how seasons are so much more than just times of the year. As a result, I've decided to personalize this coming season. We don't have to wait for a new year to set goals and make positive changes. A new month, a birthday, an anniversary, a new week, a new day and a new hour are all perfect opportunities for new beginnings.

I love to use new seasons as my markers for new beginnings because everything and everyone that comes into your life is for a season. Some seasons are longer than others but most leave you with a lesson that allows you to come out better than you were before.

This might be your season of health and wellness, your season of financial literacy, or your season of focus on family. This is my season of personal development. Whether we realize it or not, we invest so much in making other people's dreams come true, that very little is left over for our own self-improvement. Think about it. How much do you really invest in personal development?

Now when I say personal development, I don't mean getting your hair and nails done. Don't get me wrong, that is very important too. But that goes under self-care which is another subject. When I say investing in personal development I mean investing time and money into books, classes, workshops, mentors, coaches, conferences and networking opportunities that move you forward in the mission and vision that you have for your life.

We tend to invest in high-risk things where we may get little or no return, but self-investment is a win-win situation. When you invest in yourself, the return is always high. In the financial world the acronym, ROI stands for Return on Investment. This speaks to the amount that you get back when you invest in something. When you invest in yourself, the return is priceless.

This week I challenge you to invest in something for your own personal development. It can be as small as a book, or even the time it takes to read an article online that will enrich your life in some way.

Week Forty Nine

Click Refresh

One of my favorite functions when it comes to using the internet is the refresh button. According to Google, the refresh button allows a static page to update information that has been changed. As these days fold into weeks and these weeks give way to months, it is due time to click the refresh button on our lives.

Think about the things that happen when you click the refresh button on the computer...

The Current Page Will Reload and the Browser Will Look for an Updated Version of the Page...

New things appear and old things are gone. Sometimes we get in such a stagnant place in our lives, that we only see that static page. We only see what is in front of us as it is, even if it's not the correct or most up-to-date information. Let's take a long term relationship for example.

You met your mate in high school or college and they were good looking, charming, popular and had all of the potential in the world…now fast forward ten or twenty years. You are still looking at what they were, when in reality, that potential was never realized and they are still living in and on their past fame and acclaim. Do you want to see who you are really with and whether the two of you are on one accord? *Click refresh…*

Images Don't Load Until You Click the Refresh Button…

Have you ever gotten to a page that should be full of colorful images, but all you see are empty spaces and red X's? Well, when you click refresh, all of the images become visible and show clearly and vibrantly. Let's liken this to our outlook, perception and mental health. When you are depressed or caught up in that stinking thinking, you step outside and you see trash, graffiti, dirt, bums, and litter.

When you change your mindset and mood to a more positive one, you see a beautiful clear blue sky, a bright shining sun, and an opportunity to help or minister to a person in need, and a city that, despite the odds, remains resilient and has a plethora of hidden gems. Do you want to see these wondrous things?

Click Refresh…

You Can't Transmit Information Properly Until You Click Refresh...

Have you ever been trying to send an email and no matter how many times you hit the send button, it just won't go through?

Sometimes when we're under stress or duress it directly affects our ability to communicate effectively. How many times have you been having a bad day, or someone in particular got under your skin, then you go and speak to the next person you encounter in an unkind way?

Sadly, often times it is the people that we love the most that get the negative talk, complaints and argumentative dialogue. We need to dump that old information or situation that upset us, take a deep breath and treat every present and future situation as a new one. Do you want to communicate with kindness and love no matter what? *Click refresh...*

Do you feel that it's time for a positive change in your life? Click Refresh!

Week Fifty

Walking in Your Purpose Saves Lives

We were all placed on this Earth for a purpose; unfortunately, many of us have no clue what that purpose is. Out of the small number of people that do know what it is, fewer still are actually walking in their purpose. I was inspired to contemplate these concepts when I heard a wise man say something to this effect:

"Our purpose really isn't about us at all. It is about all of the other people that are supposed to be blessed by our gift."

He then went on to say something so powerful that I don't even think he realized the impact of what he said until he witnessed the explosive reaction of those that were listening.

He said, "Someone died yesterday because I wasn't doing what I knew I was supposed to be doing last week."

Let that marinate for a minute...

My friend that experienced the insight alongside me altered it even further by saying,

"Someone died TODAY because we didn't do what we knew we were supposed to be doing yesterday."

Think about it. Because you didn't write that book, or say that speech, or create that invention, or operate in whatever it is that your calling is, no matter how simple or complex...someone died.

What a way to think of things. Imagine what life would be like if Cleveland inventor Garret Morgan had never created the gas mask or the traffic signal. Think about how many lives have been saved by the powerful words of pastors, motivational speakers, and crisis hot line workers.

Some time ago I remember receiving a chain letter email about a young man that was on his way to commit suicide when an unaware stranger showed him some basic loving kindness that prompted him to change his mind. It's that simple. Your purpose may be to encourage people, spread love and let them know that they are not alone.

This week I encourage you to take some time to do some internal reflection. Reflect on that thing that you know you are meant to do. Reflect on the joy and fulfillment that it will bring you, but also reflect on the positive impact that it will have on the lives that you touch.

Pursue your passion.

Live your dream.

Walk in your purpose.

Save lives.

Week Fifty One

Be the Change You Want to See

"Be the Change You Want to See in the World"

–Mahatma Gandhi

The quote above has always been one that has resonated with me. In relationships, whether they are romantic, platonic, or with family, we have a tendency to try to change people into what or who we think they should be or what we want them to be. I'm sure that we've all learned by now that we cannot change people. What we do have the power to do is to change ourselves.

Think about how you feel when someone tells you what you need to or should be doing. Even when they say it nicely, my first reaction is often to rebel and do the exact opposite of what they are telling me to do. Constructive feedback is one thing, but lecturing someone on how they need to change is totally different and rarely well-received.

As a result I've found that the best way to see change is to be the change that you want to see.

What can you do differently to reduce or eliminate the undesirable behavior that your loved one exhibits without being manipulative?

Here are a few practical examples...

Let's say that your loved one has a smoking habit that you do not care for. Physically removing yourself when they smoke will let them know how you feel about it without you telling them that they need to quit. Telling them that they should stop does not encourage them to do so, but perhaps the absence of your presence may help them to give the idea some thought.

I've noticed that people only do what you allow them to. The cigarette smokers in my life know that I do not like smoke, but since I don't set any clear boundaries, I am still subject to this undesired behavior. But I've noticed that there are certain people that they do not smoke around. This means that the people that they do not smoke around have set some clear boundaries. Know what you want; as well as, what you will and will not accept and be firm in that.

Perhaps your issue is that you and your loved one argue all of the time. You can be the change that you want to see by making an effort to be more positive. If you find yourself being negative or reacting to their negativity, take a step back. Either counter their negativity with positivity, or simply do not respond or react to their negativity at all.

I watched the film "Fireproof" a few months ago and in the movie, the husband was reading the book, The Love Dare. The love dare is a forty day process based on biblical principles where couples are given a different challenge each day. One day the husband was given the challenge of not being negative. Even if his wife was negative he had to be silent and not reciprocate her actions. Give that a try. A person can only fuss, rant and rave all by themself for so long before they begin to feel foolish.

These are only a few examples, but I encourage you to examine the stressful situations in your relationships and think about how changing yourself can benefit the union.

Relationships, whether they are romantic, or with friends, family or co-workers, are what keep us alive, so it is important to nurture them and put in the time and effort that it takes to make them work.

Week Fifty Two

The Faith-Based Plan

Employee or Entrepreneur:
Who are You? Who do You Want to be?

I'll never forget the day when a friend of mine learned that I did not have what he considered to be a "real" job. He jokingly said, "What are you on, the faith-based plan?" He was laughing, but the more that I thought about it, the more that it made sense. I am on a Faith-Based Plan because I don't have to know where my next check is coming from to feel a peace beyond all understanding.

When I made the somewhat impromptu decision to leave my job, my employer at the time could not fathom how I could possibly survive. "What will you do for health insurance?" he asked. My response was, "I didn't even need health insurance before I started working here." That's what we often fail to realize; we jeopardize our mental and physical health more by being in environments that are not fulfilling because stress will make you sick, literally.

Now I don't encourage anyone to just up and quit a job without a plan. First and foremost you must have faith, but you must be creative in how you bring in income because whether you have a job or not, the bills still need to get paid. I have been without full-time employment for almost four years now and I have yet to be homeless or hungry. Sadly there is no longer any such thing as a safe or secure job. I feel that I am in a better position than most because my livelihood is in not in the hands of another human being. If you are contemplating taking a leap of faith, like I did, let me recommend a few basic principles that I practice.

Planning, Patience and Persistence

I am not the type to plan years in advance, but I try to plan at least a month in advance to make sure that I am able to cover my monthly living expenses like rent, car payment, and communication (home phone, cell phone and internet). I also make sure that a certain amount of money is set aside every month for self -care, investing in my vision, entertainment and emergencies.

While living on the edge like this is fulfilling beyond measure, notice that I did not say it was easy. I saw financial expert, Catherine Eagan, speak last year and she said something that really resonated with me... "Where you are right now is not necessarily representative of where you are going." You are going to be everything that you hoped and dreamed to be if you see it and you believe it, but it may not happen overnight, so patience is an absolute must.

There will be times when you can't eat what you want, there will be times when your work is rejected or criticized, there will be many roadblocks along the way, but never ever stop. That is a mantra that I tell myself constantly: Never stop. No one who is anyone ever got anywhere without being persistent. Did you know that Walt Disney filed for bankruptcy? You may not have known that, but you do know that he never gave up because, even in his absence, his legacy lives on.

Believe in You

If you don't believe in yourself and what you do, no one else will. Why should they? You train people how to treat you so if you believe that your dream is the best thing since sliced bread then trust and believe that the world will, too. Make yourself a HUGE DEAL. People often think that I spend thousands of dollars on marketing and promotions, or that I have some marketing or publicity guru behind me...the truth is that I just spend a whole lot of time believing in me. I constantly and consistently put it out into the world that I AM a HUGE DEAL, and wouldn't you know, other people started believing it too.

Get Your Legal Hustle On

When you don't know when or how your next check is coming, creativity is key. Tap into all of your talents and skills because there may be times when it feels like your true dream is not bringing in the cash that you desire. Let me give you a few examples. Over the years, I have taught myself to do hair and nails. It's not something that I am head over heels in love with doing, but trust and believe that it gave me tons of extra money during my college years. In addition to writing, there have also been times where I have taught dance and kickboxing. When I did those things to supplement my income I was still operating in my purpose of adding value to the lives of others while making some extra dollars.

The possibilities are endless...dog walking, landscaping, selling your books or artwork, freelance writing, rent parties, selling plates of food...shall I go on, or do you get the picture? When you are creative, there are tons of things that you can do to supplement your income without engaging in any questionable or illegal activity. And, in most cases, you have a ton of fun while you are at it.

Invest in Personal Growth and Development

I have been able to operate so many legal hustles because I always invest in my own personal growth and development. While it may be challenging, it's never too late to invest in a new skill.

Many classes and resources are free and readily available; we just don't take the time to do our research in order to realize that these opportunities exist.

Learning gives you the time and space to think and grow, which allows you to realize your true potential. So I encourage you to take the money that you spend at the bar, or going out to eat at restaurants, and enroll in a life coaching session or a class at a local college or university that will help you to hone your craft.

Downsize to Maximize

Sometimes in order to get ahead, you have to leave some things behind. Do you really need four different gym memberships when you barely attend any of them? That was me. I had a membership at three different gyms until I decided to start teaching fitness classes, which not only brought in extra money, but it also came with a free gym membership. As a result, I ended up saving at least $150 per month. Now that is an extra $150 that I can use to order my books to sell, or for that personal growth and development that I spoke of.

How can you downsize your life to maximize your dream? Can you move into a cheaper residence? Can you do your own hair and nails instead of going to the salon? Could you host a Girls Night In instead of going to a Girls Night Out? Think about it and adjust accordingly.

Sacrifice for Success

With success comes sacrifice. During your time of building, you may not be able to live the lifestyle that you are accustomed to. For instance, I have discovered several delicious options that I can prepare with a bag of potatoes. It goes back to being creative. You may not be able to eat how you like to eat, dress how you want to dress, or party like you want to right now, but the benefits in the not so far away future are well worth it. One of the main things that all wealthy people have in common is that they practice delayed gratification.

Sacrifice doesn't always mean giving things up. It just means adjusting the way that you do things so that it helps you to build your vision. For instance, I LOVE, LOVE, LOVE to travel. So I have incorporated that into my business. When I want to visit a city, I set up some speaking engagements, consulting work, book signings and book club appearances so that I am still bringing in income and working toward my dream, while having fun at the same time. They say don't mix business with pleasure, but why not? I work hard, so I like to play hard and as long as business is getting handled, I don't see the harm in that.

In conclusion, I want you to ponder a few pertinent questions. Are you an employee or an entrepreneur?

Are working to make someone else rich, while you make ends meet, or are you working to build your own empire?

Where are you now?

Where do you want to be?

If you are happy with being an employee, then give it your all. Give your job your energy, enthusiasm and excellence; otherwise, choose another path. There is also a hybrid approach where you are an employee, but you are also an entrepreneur on the side. If this is the case, learn to have a healthy balance and don't let one suffer because of the attention that you are giving the other.

I have chosen the path of entrepreneur. If I am to be an employee, I will be an employee of my own company. Whichever path you choose, know that living your dreams is possible. It just takes believing in you and what you do...faith and work. The Faith-Based Plan is a package that has infinite perks and benefits. Let me know when you are ready to sign up.

Book Club Guide

Anyone can form a book club around the messages in this book. My recommendation is that you get with a partner or group and commit to reading one chapter each week. Then make plans to discuss the message, preferably on Monday mornings to get your week off to a great start.

Most of the messages ask questions or pose a challenge. Use the questions and challenges embedded in the messages to guide your discussion. You may also add the following questions to guide and enhance your dialogue...

Monday Morning Motivation Discussion Questions

1. How does the topic of this message apply to your life?

2. What is one small and manageable change that you can make, related to the subject of this message?

3. What is one thing that you will change or do differently after reading this message?

4. What stood out to you about this message?

5. What supplies, materials or support might you need to meet the challenge posed in this week's message?

6. How did the application of last week's message affect your life?

7. Who is someone in your life that might benefit from you sharing this message? Why?

8. Who is someone in your life that can hold you accountable for the changes that you plan to make based on this week's message?

Mid-Year or End of Year/End of Book Reflection

9. Which message has resonated with you the most? Why?

10. What has been the most powerful impact or lasting change that has happened in your life as a result of one or more of the messages in this book?

Acknowledgements

Thank you, God, for giving me the inspiration to write these messages. They couldn't have possibly come from little ole me alone. Sometimes when I go back and read them I'm like, "Did I write that?" God, I know that you are my co-author. Thank you for using me.

Thank you to the loyal readers who have applied these concepts to their life and let me know that it helped them through the tough times and that it works. It is because of you that I wrote this book and it is because of you that I know that this matters...

Margaret R. Jones, Oscar Collins, Jarred Jernigan, Cheryl Lynn Pope, Jaylen LaGrande, Sandra Epps, Shay Love, Keitta Williams, Stephanie L. Jones, Constance Smith, Jealisha Calvert, Chris Lee, Karen Rush, Sylvia Hubbard, Stephanie Penn-Danforth, Robert Powell, Venus Mason-Theus, Nicole Ashley Allen, Shamyle Nesfield, Jah X El, Stephanie Ellis, Dustin Lane, Andre Archer, Anthony Redditt, Kwame Powell, Sandra Lawrence, Travon Talley, Venus Diva Magazine, Sole Magazine, Dimari Anderson, Cliff Chatman, Verlean Singletary, Ray John, Phette Ogburn, Monike Welch, Shai Lynn K. Davis, Lynnette Marie Jones, Caroline Shiner, Khalika Crayton, Cindy Folson, Avis Mays, Danielle Wideman, Robyne Daniels, Kimberly Mukfaria, Paulette Stanley, Natasha Lampkins, TaNisha Webb, Kai Mann, Louise Bannerman, Darrin Lowery, Tim Miller, Janice Jones, Ragu Navaratnam, Kayln Risker, Brook Blander, Karen White-Owens, Linda Davis, Kenya Whitaker-Black, Renae Phelps, Literary Ladies, Distinguished Sisters Literary Society, Motown Review Book Club, Ladies Literary Society, and many more.

This book is dedicated to my family: Mom, Dad, JR, Oscar and Lil' Ron.

Most Sincerely,
Just me...Monica Marie

171

About the Author

MONICA MARIE JONES is an author, motivator and entrepreneur. Her published works include *The Ups and Downs of Being Round* (Fiction/Self-help), *Taste My Soul* (Poetry), *Floss* (Urban Fiction), *Swag* (Fiction) and *Sweet Soliloquy* (Poetry). She has contributed to *Chicken Soup for the Girls Soul*, *New Directions for Youth Development*, 44th and *Souls of My Young Sisters*. She received her Bachelor's degree in Elementary Education from Eastern Michigan University and her Masters of Social Work from the University of Michigan. Currently she resides in Detroit, Michigan where she operates her motivational speaking, training and consulting company, *Inspirationista Ink LLC*; her publishing and literary promotions company, *The Literary Loft LLC;* and her real estate investing company, *Team JP Enterprises LLC,* along with a partner. Visit her website at **http://www.monicamariejones.com**